Cleared For Takeoff

A Pilot's Story of Challenges and Triumphs

Best Wishes
William R Norwood

By William R. Norwood

First published by Dog Ear Publishing
4010 W. 86th Street, Ste H
Indianapolis, IN 46268
www.dogearpublishing.net

ISBN: 978-1-4575-2360-1

This book is printed on acid-free paper.

Printed in the United States of America

Dedication

To Molly, for her continuous love and for making my life complete.

To my son, George, who has been an inspiration to me.

To my grandchildren Rianna, Emma, Reed and Tiffany—
may your dreams come true.

In loving memory of Bill Jr.
whose courageous spirit will always be with me.

Acknowledgments

I extend sincere thanks to:

my gracious, merciful, and loving God who is constantly by my side and to whom I give all the praise, honor, and glory.

my wife, Molly, for urging me to write this book.

my children and grandchildren for enriching my life.

my parents, siblings, teachers, mentors, extended family, and friends who have walked this journey with me.

my friends, Mike and Marianne Lawrence, whose invaluable editing expertise and advice gave this book shape and focus.

my cousin, Ethel Gibson, who read my first rough draft and is one of my staunchest supporters.

to John Hall at *Tigerhill Studios* for the use of his photo on the cover. This UA 727 landing at Meigs Field, Chicago, IL is now in the Museum of Science and Industry in Chicago.

to the *DogEar Publishing* family for making this book a reality.

Author's Note:

I have tried to relate my story to the best of my ability. The events are stated as I have recalled them and with my view of what actually happened.

TABLE OF CONTENTS

FOREWORD

Nearly two decades after Jackie Robinson integrated major league baseball, a half-dozen African American skycaps in Cleveland savored a moment they never expected in their lifetimes. They proudly greeted William R. Norwood, the first African American pilot for United, a special man who for three decades after that historic flight would make the friendly skies friendlier. Like Jackie Robinson, Bill bore the trailblazer's burden. During his 12-month probation, he endured offensive remarks from fellow pilots and a passenger who spotted him in the cockpit while boarding, spewed her racist wrath and returned to the terminal. Like Jackie and Rachel Robinson, Bill and Molly Norwood were keenly aware that they—and, yes, their race—were again on trial. But they, like Jackie and Rachel, were equal to the challenge.

Bill had become the first black quarterback at Southern Illinois University even after an assistant coach tried to coax him into a flanker slot. He had graduated from primary flight instruction school at Moore Air Force Base in Texas after being warned that no African American had made it. He had excelled in advanced Air Force training in Selma after an uneasy brush with the Klan near the bridge where John Lewis and other voting rights demonstrators were later attacked by foaming segregationists.

He had a strong foundation: Parents who both loved and disciplined him. Teachers in his all-black elementary school who set high expectations and helped students meet them. A Tuskegee airman who, as his principal and mentor, kindled his passion for aviation.

Bill rose to become the first African American captain for United. He was the first Southern Illinois University alumnus appointed to its governing board. Numerous awards attest to his success. The love for him among current and former pilots, flight attendants and skycaps across the nation speaks to his humanity. Through it all, he has coped with adversity and tragedy, including his son's death after a valiant battle against cancer.

Bill's contemporaries will relish this memoir. Even more importantly, it promises to provide inspiration and guidance to young people—especially those of color—who too often are enveloped by hopelessness. It is a great story, and he tells it with the candor, courage, wisdom, humor and grace that helped him overcome—and then some.

Mike Lawrence
Retired Director of the Paul Simon Public Policy Institute
Southern Illinois University
Carbondale, Illinois

INTRODUCTION

Why should I write a book about myself? On the surface, it may appear to be grandiose and egotistical. Many persons, including some whose opinions I truly respect, have encouraged me to put my story into print. My wife, Molly, has often urged me to attempt this endeavor. She believes every person has a story to share that could be an interesting book. However, I have staunchly opposed the idea. After all, my life has been quite simple and ordinary. After several years of Molly's urging me to write my story and her gift of voice recognition software, I thought, "Why not?"

So, I began this effort mainly for my son and my grandchildren. I hope by sharing my story and life's experiences, they will better understand and appreciate their heritage and lineage. In addition, perhaps something in this treatise will give enlightenment and encouragement to others. Dreams can come true. I believe life is about having a plan, modifying the plan when necessary, and diligently working the plan.

PROLOGUE

It was my maiden flight for United Airlines, the first by a pilot of my race to fly the Friendly Skies. There was little excitement or curiosity as I walked through flight operations at O'Hare Airport in Chicago in September 1965. No stares. No quizzical expressions. Most of United's African American employees knew through news releases and the grapevine that I would be arriving at O'Hare. However, I did not see any of the African Americans in management or supervisory positions as I made my way to the aircraft. Things were almost routine—until we landed in Cleveland.

To my astonishment, waiting for me at the arrival gate were six African American skycaps. Each one understood the historic nature of this occasion. They were all eager to see the first African American pilot with United, and they expressed how proud they were—something they never thought would happen in their lifetime. I was overwhelmed by the reception and those in attendance. Several of these men had finished their workday two hours earlier and waited for my arrival. During my tenure at United, I was fortunate to meet many of the skycaps at different airports, and I remain close friends with several of them to this day. Riley Moore, one of the men who greeted me in Cleveland, was also on my last United flight when I retired in 1996. Riley, who turned 96 in December 2012, commented on a video made for my retirement, "Bill not only spoke to us, he shook our hands, and he is my friend."

Because of what the day meant for Riley Moore and the others there, it became more meaningful for me. It was a magic moment on a journey that began in a small, segregated, southern Illinois town where I was nurtured by loving and demanding parents. I was taught in a segregated elementary school by teachers who expected the best from students and prepared us to overcome the hatred and unfairness of racism. I was mentored by a Tuskegee airman who taught me lessons for a lifetime. It has been a journey that took me to a great university that gave me the opportunity to succeed on the football field and in the classroom, to a military that challenged my survival instincts, to a world-famous airline, to a private audience with the first African American President of the United States, and to a blessed retirement that has allowed my wonderful wife and me to thoroughly enjoy our golden years. There have been many moments of struggle—especially during the illness and loss of our son after his courageous battle with cancer. However, I will never forget the other moments, including the one in Cleveland where history and everlasting friendships were made.

PART ONE

Nurtured and Challenged in a Segregated Town

"Every great dream begins with a dreamer. Always remember, you have within you the strength, the patience, and the passion to reach for the stars to change the world."

—Harriet Tubman

My family lived in the southern Illinois town of Centralia. This small town is located about 100 miles north of the southernmost tip of the state, where the Ohio River flows into the Mississippi River. This location is important because, during my formative years, southern Illinois was closer in attitude and activities to Mississippi than Minnesota. The culture in southern Illinois was discriminatory and segregated. African Americans did not have separate drinking fountains as was the case in some southern states, but there were definite restrictions on mobility and daily living. For example, African Americans could not stay in the town's only hotel or eat in the downtown restaurants. The elementary schools were segregated. I mention these examples so that, when I refer to them later, there will be an understanding of how these restrictions affected some of the situations and actions I experienced.

I was born on February 14, 1936, and I was welcomed by my parents, Sam and Allineal Norwood, and three siblings, Delores, Robert, and Mary Ann. My younger brother, Richard, was born three years later. We were all delivered at home by Dr. Percy May, Centralia's only African American doctor. We lived in the northeastern part of town in a modest, two-bedroom home. A third bedroom was added after I finished college.

My dad was a carpenter who was not allowed into the union because of the color of his skin. Consequently, his wages were below union scale. He worked for an African American contractor, Mr. John McLemore. They worked well together and took great pride in their superlative craftsmanship. But, like with most construction work, the winter months were slower, and, financially, the times were very "lean."

My mom graduated from Southern Illinois Normal College (now Southern Illinois University) at Carbondale in 1926. At that time, a student could graduate in two years with a teaching certificate. Mother taught for a few years until she and my father married. Since women could not continue to teach if they were married, she became a cook at the local Walgreens drugstore. The store had seating accommodations for 16 to 20 people, but, of course, African Americans could not eat in the store.

My memory is a bit foggy on the years prior to first grade. However, there are several things I clearly remember, and they are definitely memorable and noteworthy—the outhouse, Saturday night baths, the potbelly stove, and thawing water pipes.

We had no indoor plumbing. Our toilet was an "outhouse," and one of the best constructed in the neighborhood. It was built during the Works Program Administration (WPA). It had a concrete floor and was solidly built. To this day, I do not spend much time reading or cogitating in the bathroom, and I am sure my outhouse experiences have something to do with this. As I have explained to Molly, there are only two seasons of the year when using an outhouse is tolerable—spring and fall. One did not linger too long in the winter because it was too cold, or in the summer because of the heat and the swarming flies. I soon learned not to dawdle, but to quickly take care of business and be gone.

Saturday night meant bath time and an interesting ritual that was not always welcomed. We bathed in a galvanized, "Number two" tub. We had cold running water, but we did not have a hot water heater. Water was heated on the wood-burning stove. (Electric stoves came much later.) My oldest sibling, Delores, took her bath first, and the rest of us followed in the order of our ages. This meant that, when it came my turn at number four, the water was cold and not as clean as it was when Delores bathed. The bright side was that I was not the last—Richard had to bathe after me. As a result of these Saturday night baths, I learned the seniority system and that "rank has its privileges."

I vividly remember the potbelly stove that sat in the center of the house and provided the central heat for our home in the winter. The stove would be cherry red at times. On cold days, my family would gather around the stove, and the warmth was great on the side of the body that was facing the stove. However, the other side of the body would be cool. I learned several scientific facts because of that stove. Before going to bed, someone in the family would "bank" the stove with a big lump of coal. The damper on the stove would then be turned low so the coal could burn slowly. Our hope was that, the next morning, enough residual fire would exist to get the "banked" coal off to a roaring start. I also learned quite early about southern Illinois high-sulfur coal. Upon waking, there would be a "clinker" in the stove that consisted of ash and some partially-fused residues. This "clinker" would be about two-thirds the size of the original lump of coal that was put in the stove the night before.

When the weather was very cold overnight, the water lines would freeze because they were not buried deep enough. One of my siblings or I would go outside, set a wad of newspaper on fire, and run the burning paper along the water pipes to get the water flowing.

These reflections have revealed events that were more significant than I realized at the time. It is only now that I recognize their influence in developing my appreciation for the blessings I have at this point in my life.

Elementary School

School was a high priority in the African American community in Centralia. There was great pride in the teachers, the schools, and the graduates. Lincoln School was especially proud of its well-educated and outstanding graduates. All of the African American youth in Centralia attended Lincoln School, except for about 12-15 children who lived and attended school in an area called "south town." The competition between the schools was keen in academics and athletics, and Lincoln School competed well in both areas. All eight grades were in one building and one teacher taught most of the subjects for that grade level.

When I started Lincoln School, Mr. William Pryor was the principal. Mr. Pryor was an intelligent, bright, dedicated, and strong leader who was emulated by principals at other schools. After Mr. Pryor retired, Lincoln School had a couple of principals who allowed enthusiasm and achievement to wane. This all changed when a new principal, William Harold Walker, a World War II Army Air Corps Tuskegee Airman fighter pilot, took over the helm. Mr. Walker was in the mold of Mr. Pryor, and things began to turn around and exhibit the excellence that was expected at Lincoln School.

I can still remember all of the teachers' names at Lincoln School and the grades they taught. All of them had high expectations for each student's academic achievement and behavior. Ms. Helen Mason was the first-grade teacher who got us started very well academically and helped build our self-esteem. Second grade was taught by Ms. Delores Holden, and she carried on the tradition that Ms. Mason had established. The third-grade teacher was Ms. Bella Claybrook, who was compassionate, but stern. Ms. Edna Bibbs, the fourth-grade teacher, was extremely kind and gentle. We could get away with a lot more in her class than in the classes taught by previous or subsequent teachers. I believe we took advantage of Ms. Bibbs. However, I think all the students understood that, in the next four years, we would be getting stricter, and more demanding, teachers. Our faculty's goal was to prepare us for a successful transition to high school. Fifth grade was taught by Ms. Ozeneva Pyles Hite. She was the first of the "no nonsense" teachers we would have in the next few years. She demanded excellence in studying, accomplishments, and behavior. She also did not take any "guff" from parents.

Ms. Laura Ricks was the sixth-grade teacher, and she ratcheted up what we had learned from Ms. Pyles. She was stern and, in a businesslike fashion, indicated to each of us that she was serious from the opening bell until the end of the school day. She was a caring teacher, but she would not tolerate any nonsense. In seventh grade, we had our first male teacher, Mr. Polk. He would walk around the room with a swagger that silently indicated no one should challenge him on any issue. He walked with a limp because part of one leg was artificial. He would not tolerate either an adult or a student speaking disrespectfully to him.

The eighth-grade teacher and principal was the previously mentioned Mr. Walker. He was tough, but fair. He was also a good athlete and played basketball and softball with the students. This gave him an excellent opportunity to see what the students were like outside of the classroom. I'm sure he used this in evaluating how students would do in an unsupervised situation.

There are two things I clearly remember about Mr. Walker and the eighth grade. First, he strongly disliked students mispronouncing the word "get" by saying "git." He would reprimand students and say there is no such word as "git." Then, he would ask the students to pronounce it correctly several times. Second, all the students knew Mr. Walker could easily be diverted from classwork, particularly mathematics, if they asked him about his experience in the Army Air Corps and flying airplanes. I would always delight in the four- or five-minute diversion to hear about his experiences.

The only time I came close to getting into trouble with Mr. Walker was when a friend and I were fighting. It was not a big fight, but we were pushing, shoving, and being unruly in the classroom, and our teacher sent us to the principal's office. Mr. Walker had us sit down and said he would get back to us later. Corporal punishment at Lincoln School was totally acceptable, and a spanking with a belt for older students was the most widely-used method. My friend and I were certain this would be our fate. However, after an hour, Mr. Walker returned, looked at us sternly, and asked if we could return to the classroom and act like gentlemen. We both assured him we could. This was the closest I ever came to getting into trouble under Mr. Walker's tutelage. Waiting patiently was not easy, and it is something I still find difficult to do.

At school, we also were taught to be good citizens. This was a carryover from what we learned at home. We were told that we were representing our family, our church, our school, and our community when we were out in public. Any undesirable action reflected upon how we were raised and educated. This was something we took very seriously. If we got out of line blocks away from home, we were in trouble, and any adult could reprimand or correct us if he or she saw any inappropriate behavior. All adults were called Mr. or Mrs. We also responded to every adult with "Yes Ma'am, Yes Sir, No Ma'am, or No Sir." If we got a spanking at school, our prayer was this news would not make it home to our parents. One thing for sure, our parents would take the side of these respected teachers. There was no way to blame any of our bad behavior on anyone except ourselves. This is a lesson I am sure most Lincoln School graduates remember to this day.

Our Own Home Entertainment Center

Since financial resources were scarce, we learned to create our own fun and toys. We would make guns out of the pinewood from food crates. Sometimes, we would make repeaters on the guns by using rubber bands and a string. We pulled the string to release the rubber bands and make a repeating popping sound. We made skateboards from old skates nailed onto a two-by-four piece of wood. We had to be creative because we did not have the modern conveniences, technology, and money that most people have today.

During the winter, one of the games my brother Richard (Dickie) and I enjoyed playing was basketball in the house. First, we folded several pairs of socks together and made our ball. Then, we opened the door that led from the kitchen to the dining room to create a triangle against the wall. This triangle became our basket or goal. We would dribble by making verbal noises like "da-da-da-da-da-da" as long as possible until the dribbler needed to take a breath. Once we stopped making the noise, we were finished dribbling and had to shoot the ball into the triangle. This was not difficult because the socks were soft and they banked easily against the wall. However, my mom was not too happy because, every time the ball bounced off the wall, spots were made where dust had collected. Playing this game would entertain us for a couple of hours, because we were always trying to improve our scores. We had some very competitive games during those cold winter evenings.

Dickie and I were always trying to make racing cars like those in today's soapbox-derby competitions. We would get old lumber, a couple of axles, and wheels out of the junkyard to build our cars. Once or twice, they were pretty fancy and fast, but most of the time they were simple, crude, and slow. We never entered a competition because our cars were not constructed very well. But for a couple young lads, we were very impressed with how well we built our cars.

For me, like any other youngster, Christmas was a grand time of expectation and hope. Our family was not "flush" with money, so there were not many toys on Christmas morning. Most of the time, however, I would get at least one or two things I wanted. One of my favorite toys was a lever-action, multiple-shot, Red Ryder BB gun. I cherished that gun and I learned to fire it well. I can still relate to Ralphie in 'The Christmas Story' with his excitement about receiving his Red Ryder BB gun.

The most interesting thing about Christmas was Santa Claus. I figured out at an early age there was no such thing as Santa's bringing presents. It was hard to picture Santa Claus coming down the chimney to deliver presents because our home had no chimney. When I questioned this, it was explained that Santa came to the front door and delivered the gifts. I kept the excitement of Christmas by not letting my parents know that I knew there was no Santa Claus. As long as the gifts arrived, I played the game religiously and, I must say, some of the rewards were worth the deception.

"Double Duty" and Wisdom at the Barber Shop

In many African American communities, the barbershop is a central gathering point for dispensing and receiving information and wisdom. Centralia's barbershop was right across the street from our house. There we learned social graces, a little bit of sophistication, and, in general, philosophy about how the world operates. There were all types of discussions at the barbershop on a variety of subjects. Arguments abounded about everything. People came to the barbershop regularly. Some were getting a haircut, but most were just visiting and passing out their opinions to anyone who would listen. One man, who bought a World Atlas, would find some irrelevant fact and come to the barbershop asking if anyone knew the answer. After discussing this item for a while, he would go home, get his Atlas, and bring it back to show that he was right.

The owner of our barbershop was Bill Locke. However, his nickname was "Double Duty." The reason for this name was because he was an outstanding baseball player. When the team had a doubleheader, he would pitch in the first game and catch in the second game. He was known by this name from the first day I came to his shop until he passed away. There were two problems that one might encounter in getting a haircut from Double Duty. First, he had the old style hair clippers that pulled the hair as he was cutting it. This was long before electric clippers. This could be painful, and it was not effective in giving the most even haircut. The second problem was that Double Duty could not cut hair and talk at the same time. Consequently, what should have been a 20-minute haircut could take up to an hour. This was all part of the fun of the barbershop experience.

Double Duty's sons were outstanding athletes, and he attended most of the sporting events at the local high school. One could really keep up with what was happening in local sports at the barbershop. Double Duty knew all the players and their records, and the games would be replayed the next day at the barbershop.

Then, there were replays of the Joe Louis heavyweight title fights. On fight nights, we would bring our big Philco radio into the front yard and everyone would sit around and listen. Occasionally, someone would support the opponent of the "Brown Bomber" just to make the event more interesting. When the National Anthem was played, we would all stand at attention with our hands over our hearts. Fortunately, Joe Louis won most fights, and, when he won, it was a great evening. We looked forward to the next day at the barbershop when the fight would be replayed and everyone could get an idea of who was the best sports announcer.

Sometimes on hot, humid summer nights, my friends and I would sit on the corner and tell jokes, talk about each other, or just act silly. This was great fun and, as I look back, an education in tolerance. Someone might say something derogatory about your lineage—called "playing the dozens." We had to learn to smile or practice our verbal skills by doing the same. One soon learned "when to hold and when to fold."

On very hot nights, it would always be a treat for my brothers and me to sleep overnight on a pallet (blanket or quilt) on our front porch.

This provided some coolness on a humid night, as we had no air conditioner in our house. Plus, it gave us more space outside on a pallet than indoors with the three of us sleeping on a sofa bed (pull-out couch). These were happy times, and most of our fun and activities did not cost a penny.

Grandparents and 460 Air-Conditioning

Grandparents can have an important influence on one's life. My maternal grandparents, Edward and Tavey Humble, lived about three blocks from our home. My grandmother was called "Nana," and my grandfather was called "Pa." Although they lived nearby, I didn't spend much time with Nana and Pa. I think some of the strain between Nana and my family was because she really felt she was better than my siblings and me. Nana believed she was from English aristocracy. When I did get invited to her house, one of her favorite things was to have tea with milk in it—gag! She thought this was a classy thing to do, and she often said it made her feel like "royalty."

She was light-skinned, and, in that day and time, some people considered the lighter complexion to represent a "higher" place in "Negro" society. My grandfather, Pa, was a good man. He was a lot darker than Nana, and I always thought he was not appreciated as much by her as he should have been. However, I thought the world of Pa, and so did the rest of my family. Nana did not care for my father, and I think the feeling was mutual. Consequently, I had little interaction with Nana. I can only recall staying overnight a couple of times with Nana and Pa. Occasionally, when I visited her, she would send me on errands. It would not be unusual for me to walk 15 blocks to the store to save three cents on a pound of butter. Most of the time, my pay would be a 'thank you.' Nana was tolerated by my family, and she tolerated us, but I never felt close to her.

My paternal grandparents, Annie and Edward Norwood, were wonderful, and they also lived in Centralia. Although they divorced when I was quite young, all of my family continued to have a close relationship with both of them. My grandmother, called "Mama Annie," moved to Chicago. My grandfather, called "Da-D," was a kind, wonderful man who I always felt was in my corner. He lived with my family a few years before he died, and I have many wonderful memories of him. He wanted my siblings and me to be good young people, and he set a good example for us.

After my grandmother moved to Chicago, she married a man named Ellisward Dabner. My siblings and I spent a lot of time in Chicago. We would take the train and stay with Mama Annie for a month or so during the summer. Her daughter, whom we called Aunt Sweetie, stayed with her. Mama Annie lived in what was known as the Mecca Building, which was located on the south side of Chicago at Thirty-Third and State streets. It was a large, rectangular-shaped building that covered one square block, and it had four floors and a couple of small wading pools. The building where Mama Annie lived is near the location of the Illinois Institute of Technology and about three blocks from the old Comiskey Park.

We went to Comiskey Park for baseball games, including the Negro All-star games. These games were something to behold, as people dressed beautifully for this important event. It was unfortunate that some of the outstanding stars playing in the Negro leagues and in the All-star games never made it to the major leagues. Many of these players were overlooked until Jackie Robinson came onto the scene.

We always had a wonderful time visiting Mama Annie and Mr. Dabner because she would give us pretty much anything we asked for in such a pleasant way. But, she was also very strict, and she did not take any lip, or sassing, from any of us. We went to Chicago on the train many, many times, but after Mama Annie married Mr. Dabner, our mode of transportation changed. He had a Buick automobile and this was really something to us because my family did not have a car. In fact, my parents never owned a car until after I finished college.

Mama Annie and Mr. Dabner would drive to Centralia, pick up two or three of us, and drive back to Chicago. This was the first time I heard of "460 air conditioning." This was the situation in which all four windows in the car would be rolled down and the speed would be sixty miles per hour. Interestingly, "460 air conditioning" kept us relatively cool. However, when we put our arms out a window, bugs smashed into them just like they did on the windshield. Being with my grandparents in Chicago was a wonderful time in my life.

Public Speaking at Church

My family attended Second Baptist Church in Centralia on a regular basis. My mom was active in the church and insisted her children attend Sunday School and church. My dad did not attend, but, in his later years, he gave money to the church. Our church provided an opportunity to learn about public speaking because, starting at four years old, children were given speeches (poems) to recite in Easter and Christmas programs. I soon learned to be comfortable in front of the congregation speaking the lines I had memorized. I know some of the performances were very shaky, but the people in attendance tried to keep us motivated and always told us what a wonderful job we did. One special performance I participated in was the annual Christmas program. Bobby Joe Mason, Dale Murray, and I performed "We Three Kings." After a while, we could sing the song without having any notes or words in front of us.

Since we were required to attend church, I got to the place where I was comfortable and actually enjoyed being in the house of the Lord. I was fortunate enough to learn early that, if you have to do something, you might as well do it with a smile and make it easier to endure. Unlike some of the other churches where the youth went through confirmation classes to become part of the church, every Sunday at Second Baptist the minister would extend an invitation for people to join church. This was called, "Opening the doors of the church." If people felt like they were ready to join, they would go forward and express their decision. Later, they would be baptized by immersion.

In my early teens, the minister at Second Baptist was Rev. Owen D. Pelt. He was an excellent minister, very charismatic, projected a good image, and was interested in getting young people into the church. I decided to join Second Baptist Church. A couple of other youngsters about my age joined during that same period. We really respected Rev. Pelt, as he was helpful, supportive, and constantly encouraged us to be good citizens. However, Rev. Pelt was only at Second Baptist Church for about three years. The next minister, I thought, was not nearly the caliber of Rev. Pelt. We still went to church, but we did not have the same enthusiasm as when Rev. Pelt was the leader. This was when I learned you should go to church for your own spiritual growth, and not solely because of the minister.

"Po Devil," Pranks and Life Lessons

My best friend in these early years was Bobby Joe Mason. Like many people in Centralia, Bobby Joe had a nickname—"Po Devil." He was a year behind me in school, but he was the best athlete I have personally known. Bobby Joe and I played baseball and basketball together for several years. During this time, an African American man named

Fred Pearson was in charge of the YMCA athletic programs. Mr. Pearson was an excellent athlete in his day, and he was very helpful to all aspiring young athletes, black or white. He chose Bobby Joe and me for several of his baseball and basketball all-star teams. Although Bobby Joe was a better athlete, I was good enough to make the teams.

I really enjoyed playing on these all-star teams, especially when the games were played in the local gym because, for the first time, I was able to take a shower after the games. Although we had no indoor plumbing at home, we could bathe in a "real bathtub" when we went to Chicago to visit Mama Annie. But the showers at the gym were a novelty. (Our family added a bedroom and bathroom after I finished college.) I spent much time in the shower, which really beat taking a bath in the "number two" tub at home. Mr. Pearson treated me very well. He was also an excellent instructor in athletics, which helped me become better. Much of my athletic success, and the success of others, began in this program.

I also learned a lot from Bobby Joe. When we first started playing on these teams, we were about the same level in athletic ability. This soon changed, because Bobby Joe started practicing every day. I rested on my laurels and thought I would be as good as anyone without practicing. This was a mistake. Bobby Joe became a much better basketball player because of his work ethic, dedication, practice, and positive attitude. I remained at the same, mediocre level until I developed discipline and more athletic determination in high school. There is a saying, "Attitude is very important in determining your altitude." Bobby Joe certainly proved this to be true.

While growing up, I did my share of fighting, but the fights were mainly skirmishes and nothing of a real serious nature. If I were outclassed or outsized, I would make a hasty retreat. Now, my dad did not want me to run from fights. One day about eight blocks from home, I was jumped by a boy named Victor who was a year older than I was. He was from Chicago, and I thought he was "tough." He hit me, and I ran home. My sister Mary Ann was with me, and she hurried home and told dad I had run from a fight. When I arrived home, dad told me I should not run from a fight if the person was my size. He told me to hold my ground. I decided it was easier to go back and take a "licking" from Victor than to face dad's wrath. I went back to challenge Victor, and he did, indeed, have the "upper hand." Several days later, Bobby Joe Mason got into a fight with this bully, Victor, and was the winner. That was all I needed to boost my confidence, because I knew I could whip Bobby Joe. The next week when Victor began to taunt me, I was victorious. For the next five days, I would taunt Victor, we would fight, and I would win. Now, there was no serious fighting going on, but I wanted revenge since he had embarrassed me. And at that moment, it was sweet.

My parents were strict, but I knew my father was harsh in his disciplinary methods, and my mother was much gentler and forgiving. As I got older, I no longer got "spankings" on my legs with a switch (a long, thin twig from a tree) from mom, but I did get "whippings" with a strap or belt on my butt from dad. I had watched my older brother get into trouble and pay the consequences of his decisions. I tried to avoid entanglements with my dad and paid strict attention to what he wanted. However, being a child, I would occasionally stray from the straight and narrow and do something silly.

Halloween was always a fun time around Centralia. As youngsters, we used to do crazy pranks that today might land us in jail. One activity we did was called "chatting." Chat is very small rocks or gravel. We would get a handful of these small stones, throw them against neighbors' walls and doors and run. This would make a tremendous noise and frighten the occupants of the house. However, if someone saw us, we had to clean up the chat from their porches.

Another favorite prank, but not too bright of an idea, was to push over outhouses. There were many outhouses in our community, and we were not choosy as to which ones we pushed over. It could be a relative's outhouse as well as anyone else's. Again, the only problem was, if we got caught, we had to return and set it back up properly. The incident that stopped me from this activity was when a man was sitting in his outhouse waiting for us—with a loaded shotgun. When we pushed the outhouse over, the gun discharged. Fortunately, no one was hurt, but we were definitely scared to death.

Several homes in the white residential area of Centralia had small, black-faced jockeys holding a lantern. We did not know the story about the jockey, but we later found out that he was said to be a symbol of the loyal caretaker of George Washington's horse who had frozen in that position while he was on the job. But during my younger days, these jockeys were distasteful symbols to us. One Halloween, we decided to seek homes with these jockeys and destroy them. Most were made of chalk so they were easy to pick up, throw against the road and sidewalk, and break into smithereens.

One yard had one of these statues we really despised because it was over three and a half feet tall. We tried to pull it off its stand to no avail, because it was made of iron. We went home, got a couple of baseball bats, came back, and finally knocked it off its stand. We could not break it, so we took it to the lake and drowned the poor thing. I know now that this was destructive and unacceptable vandalism. I am certainly not proud of this action, but it felt good at that time.

The older boys in town would call us 'chicken' if we did not go with them into the cemetery. We did not want to be left behind, so we always would follow. Invariably we knew what was going to happen. When we would get halfway into the cemetery, the older boys, who were much faster, would run out and leave us in the cemetery. We scrambled to get out and find our way back home because we were afraid the graves might open and we would see ghosts. I was delighted when I was one of the older boys and could play this trick on the younger ones.

However, there were other—perhaps more profound—lessons. I was always finding ways to earn money. When I was about 12 years old, one of my first steady jobs was to deliver the *Grit* newspaper. This paper was published in Williamsport, Pennsylvania, and it arrived in Centralia Friday afternoon. I delivered it Saturday morning. The news in the *Grit* was at least four or five days old, but people bought it for the many household hints and features, not the news. Some of my customers were just being kind and tried to help me make some money. At the time, I had 33 clients. The cost of the paper was ten cents per copy. Out of the ten cents, I would keep three cents and send seven cents to "Mr. Grit." This meant I would make 99 cents a week by selling these newspapers.

One day, I got the bright idea to make this money grow. My sister Delores and my brother Bobby would gamble playing a card game called "Tonk." This game was very popular in our community. I thought I was smart enough to win some money playing this game. However, I was not as good at the game as I thought. I soon lost my 99 cents, and, then, I started to send "good money after bad." I not only lost my money; I also lost the money I was supposed to send back to the company. I was sad and started to cry because I knew I was in deep trouble. Delores told me if I would promise not to gamble anymore, she would give back the money I needed to send to the company, but she would keep my 99 cents. I thought this was a sweet deal, and I took it. This experience taught me that, in a game of chance, there is an opportunity to lose. I have not gambled in a serious way since then, thanks to my sister Delores.

My wife Molly enjoys playing slot machines, but I remind her that casinos are not built on winners. Occasionally, if we are on a cruise or if I am at a casino with her, she will give me $5 or $10, and I will play a penny slot machine. I am very satisfied with this level of gambling.

My job weeding the grass from around tomato plants taught me yet another lesson. This job entailed working in a field about 400 yards long from eight o'clock in the morning until four o'clock in the afternoon. I thought it would be pretty easy. However, after I had worked for about three hours and had finished only one-third of a row, I realized how backbreaking the work was. This labor encounter reinforced what many teachers had told me: "The better the education, the better the opportunity to have a rewarding, well-paying job." I quickly learned what real work was on hot, humid, sunny days.

You often hear the phrase, "You cannot judge a book by its cover." This became very clear to me in the following situation. In my hometown, there were several African Americans who had their own businesses. One was our physician, Dr. May. There were two grocery stores, one owned by the Downey family and one by the Burris family. Mr. Locke owned the barbershop, and Mr. Cicero Ferguson owned a successful janitorial business.

Mr. Ferguson wanted to buy a new automobile. Dressed in his clean overalls, he went to the Buick dealership in downtown Centralia. He stood in the dealership for 20 minutes, and not one salesperson asked him what he wanted or tried to assist him in any way. After obviously being ignored, he left and went to the Cadillac dealership three blocks away. A salesman immediately asked if he could be of any assistance, and, after looking at several cars, he selected a new, 1948, black Cadillac. Now keep in mind this was a time when no big markdowns existed on new cars and you normally paid the sticker price. Mr. Ferguson paid cash for the car with $100 dollar bills.

When he picked up his new car, he returned to the Buick dealership, went inside, and asked to see the owner. Mr. Ferguson told the owner what had happened earlier. He explained he felt disrespected and would never buy a Buick at his dealership. Mr. Ferguson then showed the Buick dealer his new Cadillac. When I heard this story, I realized you cannot look at a person and make judgments as to her or his educational or financial situation.

When I was about 13, my cousin, George Vaughn, and I were home alone and decided to make strawberry wine. We went to the country and picked some strawberries. We had heard about winemaking and knew we needed lots of sugar and that the wine had to "age." We put about two quarts of strawberries, three pounds of sugar, and three quarts of water into a pan and boiled and boiled the concoction.

We drained the pulp and put the juice in a jar. Because my folks would soon be coming home, the aging time for our wine was about two hours. We drank the wine while it was still warm. The wine was so sweet we both had headaches and upset stomachs. It was 20 years before I could eat strawberries. This entire process was not the smartest idea, but we both discovered the winemaking business was not for us and that we were not rocket scientists in the culinary arts.

I vividly remember the last time my dad gave me a whipping. I was 13. My dad came home from work about four o'clock, and the first thing he did was to shave before dinner, which was his daily ritual. About 4:15 on this particular summer day, I was told to run an errand for my mom to the local grocery store about eighty yards from our house. Now, it may be difficult to understand why young boys like to urinate against buildings, trees, and other outdoor things. I guess one could call it a male testosterone thing. On the way to the store, I decided this would be a good time to "wet down" a big tree that was halfway between our house and the store. I looked around, saw no one in sight, and proceeded to water the tree thoroughly. When I returned, dad asked if anything happened out of the ordinary on my way to the store. I immediately replied no. Dad again asked if I did something I should not have done on my way to the store. At this point, I knew I was in trouble, but again I said nothing happened. He bluntly asked me, "Did you pee between here and the store?" I was already committed, so I stayed with my lie. I told him no. He explained that while shaving, he looked out the window and saw what I did. Then, he said, "I am not going to give you a whipping for peeing on that tree, but I am going to whip you for lying." I took my whipping, considered myself lucky because the punishment could have been much worse, and learned another lesson. If you tell the truth, you don't have to remember what you said. This, of course, is easier said than done.

Since boxing was popular and somewhat lucrative, when I was 13, I decided to try the sport. The matches were held at the local YMCA, and boxers were divided into groups by age. Each match consisted of three rounds, two minutes each. I won my first two matches in the first round, both by a knockout. I had stiffer competition in my third match. Imagine holding heavy boxing gloves up to protect your face for six minutes as they get heavier and heavier. I won the third match by a unanimous decision. However, at the end of those three rounds, I felt as if I had been thoroughly beaten. Simply put, if winning hurt that much, I could not imagine how my body would have felt if I lost. At this point, I decided to end my pugilistic career.

Centralia was very supportive of education, and much money was spent to make sure we had first-rate supplies and teachers. Our public library was outstanding. It was a three-story building that was well stocked with great books. In eighth grade, I went to the library frequently and read many books. I stumbled upon a book that had a profound influence on my life. The book, all 800 pages, was *Don Quixote* by Miguel de Cervantes. It was a challenge for me to get through the book, but the more I read, the more I enjoyed it. It is still one of my favorite stories. Some people laughed at this simpleminded person, Don Quixote, as he tilted at windmills. We all go through life tilting at some windmills at different stages. Some of the windmills are small and ineffective, and others are monumental. The impression this book made on me is still with me today. In fighting some of my most difficult challenges, I recall this story. It's not whether you win or lose, but whether you do your best to be a fighter for a good cause. This attitude has helped me through difficult situations when the results, or the rewards, seemed bleak. The story in the book has been made into plays, movies, musicals, and other productions. To me, the whole story of Don Quixote can be summed up in the lyrics of *The Impossible Dream* written by Joe Darion for the play *Man of La Mancha*. I enjoy this song and have adopted it as my personal philosophy.

The Impossible Dream
Lyrics by Joe Darion
Music by Mitch Leigh

To dream the impossible dream,
to fight the unbeatable foe,
to bear with unbearable sorrow,
to run where the brave dare not go.

To right the unrightable wrong,
to love pure and chaste from afar,
to try when your arms are too weary,
to reach the unreachable star.

This is my quest,
to follow that star —
no matter how hopeless,
no matter how far.

To fight for the right
without question or pause,
to be willing to march into hell for a
heavenly cause.

And I know if I'll only be true to this
glorious quest
that my heart will be peaceful and calm
when I'm laid to my rest.

And the world will be better for this,
that one man scorned and covered with scars
still strove with his last ounce of courage.
To reach the unreachable star.

A Fishing Friend and a Mentor

My elementary school principal, William Harold Walker, and his wife, Viola Walker, lived one block from my family on Kell Street, but, later, they built a house on the outskirts of town. I do not know exactly when Mr. Walker took an interest in me. I remember doing chores for them and being invited to dinner at their home on several occasions. During these times, Mr. Walker would talk about fishing, hunting, and gardening. He asked me to go fishing with him, and I was delighted by this invitation. What I did not understand was there is more to going fishing than catching fish.

The night before, we would go to creek beds and seine for minnows that we could use as bait. The next morning, we would take our minnows and our fishing gear to Raccoon Lake, where we would sit high on a dam area and fish for crappie. We usually had good luck, and although crappie are small fish, we would bring them back and have a great meal. I went fishing several times with Mr. Walker, and he also took me hunting for rabbits, squirrels, and quail.

During our times together he would talk about flying, his army aviation career, and being a Tuskegee Airman. The more I heard, the more respect I had for him and all who were involved in the "Tuskegee Experiment." These times with Mr. Walker provided a great opportunity to ask questions, seek his advice, and talk about the thrill of flight. I had originally wanted to be a doctor, but my folks did not have the money to send me to medical school. After listening to Mr. Walker talk about how happy he was as a pilot, I began to edit my life's plan.

For the First Time, White Classmates

Unlike some small communities in southern Illinois that had a black high school, a white high school, and a private or parochial high school, Centralia had one high school, which was truly integrated. Centralia Township High School, with an enrollment of about 1,200, was a new experience for me. I had left an elementary school in which all students were African Americans, and my only interaction with whites had been in the seventh and eighth grades when I played on the city's youth baseball and basketball teams. When I went to high school, the school board, administration, teachers, coaches, and even the janitorial staff were all white. The facilities at the high school were excellent; the campus and the surrounding amenities were more like a university or college setting. The school's complex was composed of five buildings, some of which had multiple floors. All of the buildings were well equipped and rendered to be outstanding. The community really supported education, and the board of education made sure students had an excellent opportunity to get a quality education.

When I entered high school, I wanted to do well and get the most out of the educational opportunity. I enrolled in the college preparatory course. This unit, or education track, required four years of English, four years of math, two years of foreign language, four years of science, and three years of social studies. This provided a well-rounded education that qualified graduates to attend any university. The math track consisted of algebra, geometry, advanced algebra, advanced geometry, and trigonometry.

The science track included general science, chemistry, and physics. The chemistry lab, located on the third floor of the technical building, occupied one half of the floor and offered an opportunity for each student to conduct hands-on experiments. One day, we were conducting an experiment that involved heating sulfur in the presence of air (oxygen) until it was converted to sulfur dioxide. One student, who was behind in getting the experiment started, wound up heating the sulfur too hurriedly, and it went directly to sulfur trioxide. This caused a big cloud in the lab. Most of us had to go to an open window and get some fresh air until the air in the lab cleared up.

In other classes, such as the radio class, we actually built wireless radios that could transmit and receive communications. I had an amateur radio operator's license, and my identifier was WN9EWD. This gives you an idea of how this well-equipped school provided many opportunities for Centralia's students.

The first two years of high school went well. On the academic side, my grades were excellent, and I was making good progress toward successfully completing my college prep track. I participated in sports my first two years. While I was not a star, I competed effectively. There are two rather memorable experiences that I recall.

As a freshman playing football, I was always eager to get on the field and show my athletic abilities. The Centralia High School football team was doing very well in all of its games, winning most games by lopsided scores. One evening, we were playing an unimpressive opponent, and we were well ahead in the score and in complete control of the game. In the fourth quarter, toward the end of the game, a group of my friends and adults sitting behind our bench started calling for me to go into the game. They chanted, "We want Norwood, we want Norwood." Coach Jimmy Evers looked back at the group and finally told me to go into the game. We were on defense, and I was playing linebacker. On the first play, an opponent was tackled in the middle of the field, so I decided to join the pile—a little late—and was handed a 15-yard penalty. The coach looked back at the assembled group and said, "There's your Norwood." Of course, I was embarrassed and wanted to crawl into a hole. However, this did not dissuade me from continuing to play football.

The other embarrassment was when I was a sophomore on the junior varsity basketball team. I started the first game, and my entire high school basketball career lasted 17 minutes. During that short span, I fouled out of the game. I was using some of my football tactics in the game of basketball, which did not serve me well at all. After that one game, I decided to go to the local YMCA and play in its basketball league. In this arena, I could be a little more aggressive. The one thing required of members of the basketball and football squads in high school was participation in track and field. There is wisdom in this idea because it made me a better athlete, a lot quicker, and kept me occupied during off-season.

By age 16, I decided that I was grown enough to start smoking and drinking. Of course, neither my mom nor my dad had any idea of what I was doing. Fortunately, my experiences with both of these vices were so bad I have not indulged in either of them since.

When I first started smoking, I went to the store and got some tobacco and paper to roll my own. However, I was never good enough to roll anything that looked or tasted like a cigarette. Then, I tried picking up butts off the ground, taking the tobacco out, and rolling my own with toilet tissue, which was also a disaster. When I tried smoking dried twig "cigars" from the Catalpa tree, I ended up sucking hot air through this hollow tube, which was dangerous as well as distasteful. I soon discovered that cigarette smoke left a horrible taste in my mouth, and the smell of my breath after smoking was equally as bad. At this point, I decided I didn't want to smoke and that I did not want to date or kiss anyone who smoked.

Even after my unsuccessful winemaking experience, I still experimented with alcohol. My first encounter was a very sweet drink, called peppermint schnapps. It tasted like peppermint candy dissolved in water. It was refreshing but gave me a severe headache. Not to be deterred by a simple headache, I tried something else. I stayed away from the commercial liquors because I could not afford to buy them.

Instead I started drinking homemade wine—made by the "pros." I got sick and drunk a couple of times. One time I was so sick I could not function for most of the day. After this episode, I made a commitment to give up liquor. This was a great learning experience, and I consider myself very fortunate that drinking alcohol did not become a habit. Now, please understand that I have nothing against anyone who wants to drink. That is a choice each adult can make, and I do not sit in judgment of people whether they drink or not. It is just my decision not to drink alcohol.

A Turning Point

The summer of 1952 was a turning point in my life. I had discovered the opposite sex and had started to date. Things were going well, and I was having a great time. The problem came when I thought there were no restrictions concerning whom I dated. During that summer, several friends and I felt free enough to date white girls. The cultural norm in our community was that the races did not mix in dating, but, for us, that was in the past. Plus, we were athletes and everybody loved us. Our dating came to the attention of several community leaders, and, in their minds, this could not, and would not, be tolerated.

Although about six couples were involved in interracial dating, for some reason, four of us, two males and two females, were looked upon as being in the lead position, so we became the ones to be sacrificed to stop this "undesirable" activity. Consequently, one day, I was approached by the one African American policeman in town who asked to visit with me. I did not think anything untoward of this request. However, he took me to the police station and in an earnest way asked me if I had been involved in interracial dating. I felt comfortable with this officer because I had known him for years. I did not think he would be doing anything to get me in trouble or to deceive me into telling him something that would put me in jeopardy. How naïve I was! The result of this meeting was that the four of us were asked to refrain from attending high school for one year. Now, I do not remember if this was a request, an expulsion, or a dismissal. However, my parents did not have the financial resources to investigate, or contest, what the school board decided. The board instructed, through the principal, that we would have to stay out of school for one year. I believe they thought that if we stayed out for one year, we would stay out forever.

My parents cautioned me about making the situation any worse and told me that I should just stay out for the year and be very dedicated to return. This is one of the many times I realized that life is not always fair, since others were involved who did not suffer the same consequences. Some were star athletes, some had parents who had "status" in the community, and some were just plain lucky. None of them was asked to refrain from coming back to high school for the 1952-1953 year.

I knew my parents were not going to allow me to sit around, do nothing, not have a job, or feel sorry for myself. So my first task was to find a job. During this time in Centralia, working at the Illinois Central Railroad shops was a good job. This Corporation repaired locomotive engines and built railroad boxcars. The work was strenuous, and the biggest threat or concern about working in this environment was getting burned from the hot sparks that would fly from red-hot rivets. The job paid well, plus it was a union shop. Once a person started working there, he or she was pretty well assured of having the job for quite a while. My older brother and my brother-in-law worked in the shops, so I thought it would be easy for me to find a job there. I applied for the job and was immediately turned down. I did not realize until later that one of the managers who hired people had a daughter who was involved in interracial dating. I was thankful that I did not get the job, because the pay was so good that I might have been tempted to just work and not continue my education. I could have had enough money at age sixteen to rent an apartment, buy an old car, and live a decent life.

I was hired by the Seigler Company to spray paint the backs of stoves. I worked on an assembly line and soon learned the intricacies of the job. There were safety concerns about this spray painting operation, and, consequently, I wore a small face mask. Although I could smell the paint, I don't think it affected my health. This was a tedious and boring job, and I tried to think of ways I could make it more exciting. Only the top half of the inside backs of the stoves had to be spray-painted. The reason was the lower half was covered by parts of the stove, and no one noticed that it was unpainted. After a while, I became pretty proficient in spraying and staying ahead of the assembly line of the moving stove backs. Often I would spray paint my name on the lower half of the stove back, the part no one could see. Autographing some of the stove backs became a source of entertainment and a job I would look forward to doing each day. I was thankful Siegler did not pay as much money as the railroad shops so I would not be tempted to drop out of school.

The year's hiatus was one of trepidation and uncertainty for me. I did not know what the response would be to my expulsion. My family still loved me, my siblings still loved me, and my church family still loved me. But the feelings of the rest of Centralia's people were unknown to me. I had decided to go to work, go to church, and hope for the best. I was surprised with the positive reception from my neighbors and the community. I think I expected people to turn their backs on me. This was not the case.

The job at Siegler lasted for the entire year. This allowed me an opportunity to save money, buy some things I wanted, including my first car—a 1933 Plymouth four-door sedan. I was really proud of this fifty-dollar purchase. This was during the time when wire wheels, or imitation wire wheels, were very popular. This old Plymouth had real wire wheels. I learned how to take care of the car and handled it with extreme care.

During this year out of school, I continued to play baseball with an all-star team in the community. I worked diligently at becoming a better, smarter, more disciplined, and thankful person. No question existed in my mind, nor in my parents' and siblings' minds, that I would be going back to school and taking any criticism or any ostracism I might encounter.

Although the community support had been tremendous, I was a bit uneasy about what the reception would be when I returned to school. However, my determination to get an education made my decision easier, and I was ready to face any antagonism displayed toward me.

Before returning to school, I had to decide whether I would go out for the football team. Many in my community thought Jimmy Evers, who was the football, basketball, and track coach, was prejudiced and that he discriminated against African American athletes. Recalling the criticism I received my freshman year from Coach Evers, I did not know how the coach would react when I returned. But when everyone trotted out for the first day of indoctrination to football, I went along to claim my rightful place on the team. I had lost a year, but two of my friends, Bobby Joe Mason and Roland Burris, were very supportive and encouraged me to go back to school and to play football. To my pleasant surprise, when I arrived at the football field, Coach Evers welcomed me. We began practice, and none of the players appeared to have any concern about my being a member of the team. This initial transition back to football made it easier for me to attend classes.

(I must share the following information about my friends Bobby Joe and Roland. Bobby Joe was an outstanding basketball player at Bradley University in Peoria, Illinois. After college he was a member of the Harlem Globetrotters. Roland was the first African American elected to a statewide office in the state of Illinois, first as Illinois Comptroller and later Illinois Attorney General. He ended his political career as a United States Senator from Illinois.)

Success in the Classroom and on the Gridiron

Once I had been accepted by the football team, it was time to go into the classroom. I was worried, but I went to school as if it were just a normal day. Of the four of us who had been suspended, I was the only one to return to school. I was apprehensive about returning, simply because I did not know what the reaction would be from teachers and staff. I continued in the college preparatory track, so I was taking math, English, German, and other required courses. I kept my nose to the grindstone and kept a low profile for quite a while. However, being in sports made me more visible, and, to my surprise, there were no stares or negative comments about me or my expulsion.

My daily routine was to go to school, practice football, and go home for the rest of the day. I put much energy into studying and making sure I was excelling in academics. I had not lost my enthusiasm for learning, so getting back into the classroom was a cinch for me. The football season went rapidly and, as usual, the team was successful. During my junior and senior years, we lost only one game each year, and both losses were to East St. Louis, which had an excellent team. However, within the South Seven Conference, Centralia High School was also outstanding.

Big Money at the Bowling Alley

After the football season, I got a job at the local bowling alley setting pins. For those of you who are accustomed to everything being automated, setting pins in a bowling alley may be a foreign concept. Today, machines collect the bowling pins from the pit, put them in the rack, and send the ball back to the bowler for the next bowling sequence. However, during my high school era, everything was done manually. The bowling alley where I worked had seven lanes, and I worked two of them at a time. When the pins were knocked down, I first picked up the ball and put it on a rack to be rolled back to the bowler. Next, I would pick up the pins and put them back in the rack for the bowling to continue.

Setting pins in the bowling alley was the first time I came into a job situation of seniority. I was paid seven cents for every game I worked. If I worked more than 900 games a month, I received a three-cent bonus for every game. For example, if I worked 1,000 games in a month, I would receive $70 during the month by getting paid each week. At the end of the month, since I had set 1,000 games, I would get a $30 bonus. The way the seniority system worked was that the person who set the most games for the week would have his choice of days and alleys for the next week's schedule. The ideal situation was to work two alleys at one time, and the best nights to work were Monday through Friday. The reason for this type of schedule was that most league bowling took place on these days. League games were faster, and the bowlers more proficient, which made the evening go by fast for the pin setters. Normally, there were five bowlers on each team, for a total of 30 games for each league competition. The first games would begin at 7:00 P.M. and would end about 9:00 P.M. The second league started about 9:15 P.M. and would go until 11:15 P.M. This meant that, on good nights, Monday through Friday, I could work a total of 60 games per night. With the bonus, that would be a total of $6.00 per night. The most games I set in one day occurred during a tournament on a Saturday. I worked from 11:00 A.M. until 10:30 P.M., and I set pins for 117 games and made $11.70. This was considered "big money." I soon made it my goal to set the most games each month so I would be first on the seniority list for choosing which days and alleys to work for the next month.

My main leisure activity during the winter was hunting with my dad and sometimes Mr. Walker. I could never shoot a shotgun well, but my granddad, dad, and my older brother Bobby were all excellent shooters. I was derided all the time about my lack of accuracy and quickness to pull the trigger. I was able to get a few rabbits, so I was happy with my hunting prowess. They all tolerated me and tried to teach me how to shoot better. However, it was not until I was much older that I became a better shot. We were hunting not to kill innocent animals, but to put food on the table. Yes, we ate rabbits prepared in a variety of ways. Today, one can go to a fancy restaurant and order "hasenpfeffer," which is plain old rabbit. During that time, there was no limit to how many rabbits you could kill per day. One day, my dad killed 52 rabbits, which was a record for anyone in our neighborhood.

When spring rolled around, I was still working at the bowling alley, but I was also on the high school's track team. I was not fast, and I did not like distance running, so I became a 440-yard sprinter. I say sprinter, but, in those days, it was called a run. I would get behind the pace setter and stay within striking distance, and when I got to the last 70 yards or so, I would run as hard as I could. This worked for me. I was never a great runner, but I was competitive enough to occasionally win a first-, second-, or third-place ribbon.

A Real Job and a Tryout with the Redbirds

Summer came and I was in need of a "real" job making more money than the bowling alley offered. I knew I wanted to go to college after my senior year, and I knew I would have to pay for college myself. Mr. McLemore, who was my dad's boss, hired me to help him and my dad with his construction business. My dad wanted me to work very hard, but Mr. McLemore would always give me an easier, less strenuous job. If Mr. McLemore needed something from the lumber yard, he would give me the keys to his car, and I would run the errand. He would tell me not to hurry because he did not need it immediately. This did not always sit well with my dad, because I was able to take a break when he wanted me to be working continually.

One of the hardest jobs that summer was putting shingles on the roof of an old house. When Mr. McLemore and my dad were on the roof nailing the shingles, my job was to bring the shingles up the ladder to them. On a hot summer day, asbestos shingles can become very soft and difficult to manage. Consequently, when there was a roofing job to be done, we began at 6:00 o'clock in the morning and worked until noon. My summer job paid well, and I was able to save some money.

During the summer, I went to St. Louis for baseball tryouts with the Cardinals. I did well and was promised an opportunity to play in their system, probably D-league ball. I was a 'good glove,' and I played shortstop. In fact, some of my friends used to say I "covered the field like the morning dew." My biggest drawback was not being a good hitter. I had formed the habit of swinging late to hit the ball to right field. The problem was that I ended up swinging at fast balls after they passed the plate. I soon concluded that baseball was not a good career path for me and that playing D-league baseball was not a good way to earn a living. I decided to finish school and concentrate on football and track.

Senior Year: Football and Slurs from the Stands

The summer went fast, and, before long, I was back to football practice and my senior year of high school. The coach changed my position from flanker to quarterback. In football, Centralia ran what was called the single-wing formation. In this particular formation, the quarterback was used for catching passes and blocking. Bobby Jo Mason was the tailback and did most of the passing. I only remember throwing four passes during the season. We normally started the season with Salem, and the second game was with Flora, Illinois. Playing these two teams was like having a scrimmage since we were always the strongest of the three teams. The first time I ever recall my dad coming to a football game was the first game in the 1954 season. It was a home game, and he came with his good friend, Double Duty. The first kickoff went to Bobby Joe. We reversed, and he handed the ball to me. The deception of this play was so great that all the players on Salem went after Bobby Joe. I took the ball and went down the right sideline for a touchdown. As I approached the end zone, to my pleasant surprise, Double Duty and my dad were standing in the end zone cheering. This was a real thrill because dad had never been to one of my athletic events. We traveled to Flora for our next game. As our team came out of the tunnel beneath the stands before the game, a young white boy was counting loudly enough for all of us on the team to hear. When we finished running out on the field, he said, "They have sixteen Niggers on their team." We all thought, you have just made it very difficult for your team today; then we proceeded to play our hardest and beat them by a score of 50 plus to zero.

In the spring of my senior year, I was on the track and baseball teams. This was the first year Centralia High School had a baseball team. The final weekend of the track and baseball season was particularly exciting. One afternoon, Bobby Joe and I played in the sectional baseball tournament in Salem. After the game, we were driven to Collinsville to compete in the sectional track meet. Bobby Joe was a pole vaulter and high jumper, and I anchored the mile relay team. Bobby Joe qualified for the state tournament in his events. My team ran second to East St. Louis and qualified for the state championship. At the state tournament, the other teams were really good. Although we broke our school's record for the mile relay at the sectional, we were soundly defeated in the state tournament. This ended my high school sports career.

Bill's parents, Allineal and Sam Norwood, on their 50th wedding anniversary.

Bill in third grade.

Bill and his siblings Delores, Robert, Mary Ann, Bill, Richard

PART TWO

The SIU Years

"Hold fast to dreams, for if dreams die, life is a broken winged bird that cannot fly."

—Langston Hughes

The last two years of high school went better than I had expected. My academics were good, and I was proud of my ranking because of the intense prep courses I had completed thanks to the great teachers in my classes. Athletics had gone well, and I had been elected to the student council. I was now more inspired than ever to go to college and complete my education.

Four universities were interested in having me play football for them—Tennessee State University, Maryland State University, Bradley University, and Southern Illinois University. My first college visit was to Tennessee State University in Nashville in the spring of 1955. The coaching staff received me warmly and showed me around the campus. The tour was wonderful, and the food was excellent. During a visit to the football field, I discovered that many of the football players had returned from the Korean War to get an education and play football. These big, strong men wanted to play football very much. I looked at the muscled specimens and realized that I might be in the wrong sport since I weighed only 135 pounds.

The coach also wanted me to start practicing immediately. Now, the National Collegiate Athletic Association (NCAA) was not as strict as it is today. When I explained to the coach I had not completed all of my high school work, he told me he wanted me to start practice as soon as possible and would send for my high school diploma. I did not think this was a great idea. Later, I watched the women's track team. During this time, the Tennessee State University women's track team, the Tigerbells, was well known. When I realized I could not outrun any of the women on this outstanding track team, I decided Tennessee State was probably not the place for me to play football. I thanked the coach for his hospitality, returned to Centralia, and eliminated Tennessee State University.

While trying to decide which university to visit next, my sister Delores went into action. I do not know how it happened, but she got in touch with one of the football coaches at Southern Illinois University in Carbondale (SIUC). She told him I was interested in coming to the University and playing football and needed a summer job. The next thing I knew, I was on the phone talking to the coach about football at SIUC. I was offered a scholarship and a summer job. The job was working with youngsters who were learning a variety of outdoor skills. The camp was called 'Little Grassy.' This job paid well and provided good food. Many of the University's athletes worked at this camp. The summer went fast and, in mid-August, I started football practice.

The football team's record had not been good for several years, and a new coaching staff had been hired by the University. The head coach was Al Kawal, and the assistant coach was Carmen Piccone. Practice was all business. We practiced twice a day in the hot, humid, southern Illinois heat. I met many good ballplayers from all over the nation. Most of them had been stars in their local schools and had played for championships. There were several from the St. Louis area who had been very good high school football players. The new athletic director at SIUC was Dr. Donald ("Doc") Boydston. He had been at the University of Mississippi and came to Carbondale to be the Chair of the Health Education School and acting athletic director.

Doc Boydston was instrumental in recruiting several very talented African American football players from the south. One player, Carver Shannon, from Corinth, Mississippi, was an outstanding running back, and we soon became good friends. Five players from my high school football team were also on the SIU team. Four of us received scholarships, and three played on the first team for all four years. It was great to have these familiar faces while going through the paces and challenges of collegiate football.

Although I continued to play offense and defense, football at SIU was much more serious than in high school. One time, during practice, I was playing defensive cornerback. Ranette Lewis was a running back who outweighed me by about 45 pounds. Ranette came around the end, and I was knocked out when I tackled him. I was only out for about five seconds, but I did see stars. At that moment, I thought if I had the money I would quit the game. Instead, I recovered quickly and got back into the fray. Coaches love to see this attitude because they wanted players who have the moxie and dedication to hang in when things get tough.

I was nervous about how difficult the academics might be at SIU. I registered for math, chemistry, English, and a foreign language. Since at one time I was interested in becoming a doctor, I decided to major in chemistry because I felt it was a related field of study. I had wonderful professors in all of my courses, and the chemistry faculty was outstanding.

During this time, the University was on the quarter system, and my grades for first quarter grades were good—I received three A's and two B's. I think I worked so hard because I had a fear of academic failure and having to return to Centralia. Along with my football family, I made many friends and enjoyed life and being a Saluki (an Egyptian running dog and the SIU mascot).

Dr. Delyte Morris was President of the University and was dedicated to inclusion and fair treatment of all students. I met him my freshman year, and we had a friendship that lasted until his passing in 1982. The campus was integrated, but segregation was prevalent in the city of Carbondale. African Americans were not welcomed in restaurants, in some retail establishments, or on the first floor of the local movie theater. Ironically, African American athletes got free tickets, but were required to sit in the balcony. I only went to the theater once.

The spring quarter was a busy time. I had spring football practice and academics to conquer. I was doing well in all subjects except English. My instructor was a graduate assistant, and we did not have the best relationship. Each week the class had to write a theme. The grading system was A through F. I received an E- on my first theme, an E on the second, and an E+ on the third. Now, keep in mind an E is next to F—which is flunking. The previous two quarters I had received grades of A for each quarter from professors who were known to be tough. After the third poor grade, I went to see my instructor. The assigned topic was "Women's Hats" and I had taken a critical swipe at women's hats in general. The instructor explained that, although my theme was grammatically correct, he disagreed with and disliked the content of my paper. In a show of anger and lack of respect for this graduate assistant, I told him if I got another failing grade, I would throw him out of the window located on the third floor of Old Main. I was not proud of my behavior, and I am certainly not bragging about my threat, but I did not get another failing score on a theme and received a C for my final grade.

The First Black Quarterback

Gerry Hart, the first-string quarterback was graduating, so there was a competition to see who would be the starting quarterback in the fall. Since I had not thrown the football much in high school, my passing motion was lacking. Gerry took me aside and showed me how to throw properly. I worked on my passing technique the entire spring season. I had good coaches and practiced throwing the football and becoming a better passer.

I think one of the things that helped me in high school and college football was that I learned the different play formations easily. Before spring ball was completed, I was the number one quarterback on the depth chart. This was a very pleasant surprise to me. I think it was a shock to some members of the coaching staff who were not as excited about an African American being quarterback as was the head coach and backfield coach. In fact, one of the assistant coaches came to me and said, "Bill you have such speed and good hands, you should be a flanker back or split end." I wanted to get an education, so I would have changed positions and done what this coach suggested. However, my backfield coach, Carmen Piccone, put his arm around my shoulder, and said, "Bill you do not know what he's trying to do, but I do. If you stop being my quarterback I will take your scholarship." This was the kind of support from the coach that made me want to excel. The head coach was also fair. What he wanted was to put the best team on the field, and he felt that, under my leadership, it would happen.

In addition to athletics and academics, I was elected to the student council and appointed to the student social senate. I felt good about the year just completed and went home for a great summer. I worked daily with my dad and Mr. McLemore, saving money and having fun. I knew I had to work diligently to become a good quarterback and to stay first string at the varsity level. So, every day after dinner—except on Sunday—I would practice throwing the football. I had several youngsters, 12 and 13 years old, who would go with me to Franklin School yard. For several hours, I would throw passes to them, sometimes knocking them down. I became a better passer. I have often said that the names of these young boys who helped me learn how to pass a football should be on my diploma right along with mine. I was looking forward to the upcoming football season, since I would be the starting quarterback unless something unexpected happened.

Chemistry on the Field and in the Classroom

When I returned to SIU for my sophomore year, I was excited to get back into the swing of things. Since I had a good year academically and athletically as a freshman, I was very comfortable in my own skin. I was the starting quarterback if I continued to work hard at my craft, and that allowed me to put a little swagger in my step. Practice was going very well, and I was reinforcing my position as leader of the team. One simple statement from Coach Kawal was music to my ears. He told the team there was only one field general—the quarterback, and all others were privates. This declaration made it easier for me to deal with, and try to lead, some of the older players. A few of them did not like this proclamation, but the coach's admonition, and his actions, supported what he communicated to the team. The first two weeks of practice, I participated in full drills including tackling. After these two weeks, the coach instructed all players to refrain from tackling "his" quarterback. This really brought a smile to my face, since I would not be tackled and abused during the whole practice season. Football was fun, and the team improved upon the previous year's record by having 4-5 season. This was not outstanding, but it was going in the right direction. The coaching staff was pleased with the team's progress.

When the academic year began, I continued to do well in all my courses. I got to know my instructors better and formed bonds with them, particularly those in the Chemistry Department. There were four outstanding, nationally-known professors in the Chemistry Department who were reverently referred to as the "Four Horsemen." They were Drs. Kenneth Van Lente, Robert Scott, James Neckers, and Talbert Abbott. One of my favorites was Dr. Van Lente. He had doctorates in chemistry, physics and math. He was informal in his relationship with students. I always called him "Doc," and he always referred to me as Bill. This relationship with him, and several other professors, lasted well beyond my graduation. When I returned many years later, there was still a bond of friendship and respect between us.

During the first two years of college at SIU, each male student had to participate in Air Force Reserved Office Training Corps (AFROTC). The classes in this course were every Tuesday and Thursday morning and consisted of some classroom work, but mainly there were drills and marching routines. We were required to wear uniforms made of heavy surge wool. The drills normally were at nine o'clock in the morning. After class, most cadets hurried to get out of their uniforms. I was different. I wore my uniform all day on those days. I did not have many clothes, so this gave me two days when I did not have to worry about what to wear. Another positive about these first two years of AFROTC was that I learned more about the military and its advanced programs.

One particular program piqued my interest. For students who were serious about going into the Air Force, the Air Force would pay for 36 hours of flying time if they enrolled in advanced AFROTC, did well, and wanted to go into pilot training later. Since I had given up the idea of going to medical school, I was leaning toward becoming a pilot in the Air Force. I discussed this with my parents and Mr. Walker. My mom was not excited about my taking flight training; however, as usual, she supported my decision. Mr. Walker was elated. So, I signed up for advanced AFROTC starting my junior year.

Social life was better my sophomore year, and I began to date a very attractive African American girl. This pleased my mom, and she also urged me to join a fraternity. I pledged Kappa Alpha Psi, went to a couple of meetings, but eventually decided not to become a member. I was living off-campus with several other athletes, and we had our share of parties, so I did not feel the need for any additional social life.

Dance Floor at Night, Gospel Next Morning

When the 1956-1957 school year was over, I went home to work, throw footballs, have fun, and enjoy the success of my first two years of college. The summer was exciting. Some of the big events in my hometown were the dances held in the Elks Club that featured well-known bands from around the area. The Elks Club was located above a tavern. It had 16-foot ceilings, and there was only one way in and out, and that was up and down some very narrow stairs. My dad was secretary of the Elks and was in charge of the dances. I was hired to clean up after the big dances to make some extra money. Two of the performers were Ike and Tina Turner. Of course, this was long before they became stars, but there was no doubt that they had tremendous talent because they gave an outstanding performance.

Another memory about these late night dances, or any activity on a Saturday night, is that, no matter how late we stayed up, church was still a requirement on Sunday morning. In fact, while at SIU, even after a hard game and a night of partying, many athletes, including me, attended Hopewell Baptist Church on Sunday morning. I still remember some of the messages from the minister and the outstanding singing.

Life as a Junior: Haircuts, Mentoring, First Flight

In August 1957, my junior year started like my previous two years – with me immersed in physical training and football practice. I was entrenched as the first string quarterback and team leader. Thanks to "Doc" Boydston, our team had acquired two outstanding players from

Booker T. Washington High School in Memphis, Tennessee—Willie Brown and Houston Antwine.

This year, the team decided that an "S" should be cut in the hair of all the new players. Now, Houston Antwine, who was six-feet, three-inches tall and weighed 250 pounds, was not excited about this activity. As the leader of the team, I was selected to persuade Antwine to allow the "S" to be cut into his hair. I suggested that, if he would allow me to do the job, I would make sure it would be a "pretty S" and not mess up his hair. He grudgingly agreed, and, I must admit, I did a good job. The year ended with a 5-4 record, and it was considered a successful season.

In the late 50s, freshmen came to campus for orientation a week prior to the beginning of school. Since the football team was also on campus at this time, it gave us the advantage of checking out new students. Many of the athletes would go to the Student Center and try to impress the young women with their celebrity status. One day, when I got to the Student Center, I saw a young lady named Norma Jean Morris. I had known Norma, because she and her older sister came to Centralia in the summer to visit their aunt. My friend Bobby Joe and I thought they were very attractive and tried to visit them at their aunt's house. Interestingly enough, the minute we would arrive to visit, their aunt would suddenly appear and send us away. It was obvious she did not want us around her nieces. Ironically, their aunt encouraged visits from my classmates Roland Burris and Conrad May. Maybe it was because their fathers were an entrepreneur and a doctor, respectively.

When I saw Norma at the Student Center, she was with her lifelong friend, Molly Frances Cross. I knew they would be impressed with me as a football star and quarterback of the team. What I failed to understand was that Norma and Molly had attended a small high school in Mounds, Illinois, that did not have a football team. They had no idea of my position or stardom, and I lost all the leverage I had to elicit their attention. However, I enjoyed meeting and talking with Molly, and it was great seeing Norma again.

Through the year, I ran into Molly several times. We became friends, and I helped her with difficulties she was having in chemistry. In working with Molly, the disparity in the educational resources between our high schools was obvious. I had access to an up-to-date, comprehensive chemistry lab, and Molly's chemistry consisted of a Bunsen burner on the teacher's desk, some hydrochloric acid, sodium hydroxide, and litmus paper. This is not the array of equipment and chemicals that is necessary to learn chemistry. Consequently, her understanding of chemistry was minimal. Although I had a girlfriend, I liked Molly as a friend and was happy to help her with chemistry and other subjects. When the football season was over, I had more time to help her, and I really felt like a mentor. Our relationship changed over the next year, but more on that later.

A tragic incident happened during my junior year to a dear friend named Bob Batura, who happened to be Caucasian. He was a flanker and split end on the football team and from a fairly affluent family in the Boston, Massachusetts area. He had an Ithaca shotgun and had lent it to me for hunting when I went home. Bob wanted to visit my home and see Centralia. Now, keep in mind, my home was very basic with no indoor plumbing, no automobile, but much love. I must say I was embarrassed to take him to my home. Bob insisted he wanted to go, and, one weekend, we made the trip to Centralia. When we arrived, he told my parents how happy he was to be in our home, and he was treated well by my family. He used the same facilities I used, and we had a great time going to the local hangouts. Before we went back to the University, I returned his gun. About two weeks later, he and a couple of other football players decided to play a prank on their roommate and "short-sheeted" his bed. When Bob's roommate came home, he was angry and agitated about what they did to him. He took my friend's gun, starting shooting, and killed Bob. I often think if I had not returned Bob's gun, this tragedy might have been avoided. Bob was a gentle and honorable person, and I feel fortunate to have had him as a friend.

My year went well in academics, social life, and the AFROTC program. I was now in advanced AFROTC and had accrued several positive perks. One of the most obvious was the opportunity to shed old, heavy, wool uniforms, and don new, tailor-made gabardine ones. My classmates and I now had cadet officer rank, and the freshmen and sophomores in uniform were required to show proper respect to us, including saluting us.

The highlight of this year was my first flight in an airplane. To expand our interest in flying, the Air Force provided a 40-minute flight in a four-seat, single-engine plane called a Navion. By the time we landed, I was completely enthralled with this new adventure, and it confirmed my decision to become a USAF pilot. While still in high school, I started building plastic model planes and hanging them in the house. Next, I tried building rubber band-powered airplanes and later plastic planes powered by small engines. This was my first venture with "U-control" models. The first serious "U-control" plane I bought was a used model. I had no one to help me learn to fly such a plane, and I was never successful in flying this highly-maneuverable, complex, acrobatic, model plane. Having my first flight in the Navion was the epitome of my aviation endeavors to that point.

ROTC Summer Camp and a Beckoning Barf Bag

The summer between my junior and senior years was a carbon copy of my previous summers except for a four-week AFROTC summer camp. Mom and dad seemed very pleased with me because I was progressing steadily toward a college degree. Now, I was not the first in my family to get a college degree; as I mentioned earlier, my mom had graduated from Southern Illinois Normal Teacher's College with a two-year degree. She inspired me so much, not only to go to college, but to do well and graduate.

Working with my dad and Mr. McLemore enabled me to work before and after summer camp. A friend and I drove to Webb Air Force Base in Big Springs, Texas, located in the Texas panhandle. It was very hot and had a desert atmosphere. This is the only place I have been where the weather teletype had the abbreviation RMB, which meant "raining mud balls." This phenomenon happens when a dust storm precedes a thunderstorm, and everything exposed to the rain ends up muddy. I swear the tallest tree on this base was only six feet.

This camp was designed to give the advanced AFROTC students a taste of basic military training. It was described as a three-legged stool composed of academics, military training, and physical activity. The typical day started with vigorous physical activity, military science training from about nine o'clock until three, and competitive physical activity in the afternoon. The military encouraged competitive sports, and I actively participated in volleyball, flicker ball, track, and softball. Each day of camp was busy and provided many unimaginable experiences.

The highlight of summer camp was a ride in a T-33 jet. This airplane was a two-seater with the pilot in the front seat and the student in the rear. The purpose of this flight was to take us through several maneuvers to see how we reacted to the experience. My flight was scheduled after dinner on a very hot and humid day. The temperature was 90 degrees, and the humidity was around 80 percent. I vividly remember the dinner meal of spaghetti and hot dogs. Anxious to get to the flight line, I ate rapidly, gobbling down the food. I received the standard briefing from the pilot. A barf bag, similar to the ones on airliners, only bigger, was provided in case it was needed. Since oxygen masks would be used for the entire flight, if you barfed into the mask, you had to clean it. So, all of us student cadets were afraid we would get sick on the flight and have to clean the mask, which would have been an interminable task.

Even though there was air conditioning on the airplane, by the time we got to the runway I was already sweating. It was an exhilarating feeling when we leaped into the air. Before the flight, it was also explained how, in order to avoid getting sick, we should tighten our stomach muscles just before a serious maneuver. So, from my rear seat, I would observe the pilot making clearing turns before a maneuver and would tighten my stomach. This worked and I went through this 75-minute flight with no problems. Flying back to the airport, I was proud of myself because I conquered this flight in great condition without using the barf bag. As the pilot turned onto the final approach and was about 1,500 feet above the airport, he made a 60-degree banked turn to the left, pulling about three G's, and then rolled out. The plane was doing about 250 miles per hour when the pilot started this turn. I was not prepared for this type of maneuver, and when he banked and started to pull the G's, I felt half of my hot dog come into the mask. The fortunate thing was, because I had not chewed my food well, when the hot dog came out, it was in one piece and relatively "clean." I just swallowed it and acted as if it never happened. We landed, and I climbed out of the airplane with the pilot who was unaware of my "almost" accident. The ride was great and it solidified my decision to be a jet pilot.

For the uninitiated, "one G" refers to the force of gravity. When a plane makes a rapid ascent or a rapid change of direction, "G forces" greater than "one G" are experienced by the passengers. For example, in a steep turn, crew and passengers may experience a force of as much as "three G's" or more. The other memorable incident at summer camp related to my being a little stubborn and quick-tempered. It was the last week of camp, and I was pleased with my success in all areas of the challenging course. All students carried a little book in which they recorded when they received merits for positive actions and demerits for actions that were not so good. I had seven demerits, but most of my colleagues had that many more than that, so I felt like I was doing well. One day I was standing in the meal line patiently waiting for dinner when a regular officer, who happened to be a First Lieutenant, cut in front of me. I was a bit irate and asked him why he was cutting in line when I had been waiting patiently. He looked at me disparagingly, asked for my merit book, and gave me 10 demerits, bringing my total to 17. Since this was the final week, the importance of what he did is evident, since anyone with more than 10 demerits after graduation had to walk one-half hour, with a full backpack, for each demerit. This meant that, even if I didn't get another demerit, I would be walking for three hours and 30 minutes after graduation. I was angry with myself for reacting as I did.

The positive in all of this was, with each victory in volleyball, softball, or track, each team member received two merits. My softball team had four games remaining before graduation. As I mentioned earlier, I was a good baseball player. At camp, I was captain of the softball team and had pitched several successful games. So, I asked the team to allow me to pitch the last four games. They agreed, we won all four, and I received eight merits. This left me with nine demerits and allowed me to graduate without the punishment of walking for hours. I would like to say that I never let my temper get me in trouble again, but that would definitely be a lie. I did, however, successfully complete summer camp and received several awards, including "Captain of Softball Championship Team" and "Webb AFB Field Day Champion Outstanding Participant."

Dramatic Victories and A Prophetic Racist Remark

I headed back to SIU for my senior year and final football season. Our team was expecting a good season since most of us had been together for two or three years and had learned each other's habits, abilities, strengths, and weaknesses. We got off to a good start and ended the season with a 7-2 record, which brought the crowds and enthusiasm back to SIU football.

A notable incident happened this season. When on the football field, unlike the basketball court, it is often difficult to tell the culture or race to which a player belongs. During the first game of the season, at one point in the game when I removed my helmet, my sister Delores, who was sitting in the stands, overheard a person near her say, "They have a Nigger playing quarterback, pretty soon they will be flying airplanes." When she told me this, we were profoundly disgusted that this racist attitude was displayed so publicly. This statement turned out to be very prophetic, and I will always remember this caustic remark. It served to make me more determined to accomplish my goal of having a career as a jet pilot.

One of the highlights of the year occurred during the game against Western Illinois University (WIU). They had beaten SIU in football for the past 10 years. The stands were full, and fans were hoping we would change this losing record. At halftime, SIU was leading 24-7. Our star halfback, Carver Shannon, had gotten hurt, but we were confident when we went back on the field. In the last minute of the game, WIU was leading us by the score of 31-24. Many of our supportive students and fans had left the stadium. I received the kickoff and ran it back to our 33-yard line. Twenty-five seconds remained in the game. The WIU team knew we had to pass in order to move quickly down the field. One of our star flankers was Lane Jenkins. Lane called himself "Night Train" after the famous National Football League player, Richard "Night Train" Lane. I told Night Train to run a "down, out, and go" pattern. He was on the right side of the formation. Being a seasoned quarterback, I first looked to the left, then to the right, only to find my star flanker out of bounds. Since I called most of the plays, I called timeout and asked Night Train what happened. He explained he had run into one of the defensive players and was knocked out of bounds. So in my classy way, I told him to do whatever was needed to run the pattern as directed. I may have used a few expletives in the process. When I later listened to a replay of the game, the radio announcer said, " Fifteen seconds left in the game, and the Salukis have 67 long yards to go for a touchdown." I got the ball from the center, looked left to throw off the defensive backs, looked down field and spotted Night Train streaking toward the center of the field at about the 25-yard line. He was slightly behind the defenders and I threw the ball as far as I could, about 65 yards. He caught it on the 10-yard line and went in for the touchdown. Then, the score was WIU 31, SIU 30.

This was the first year of the optional two-point conversion in college football. We had not made an extra point so far in the game. We had to decide whether to try to kick the extra point and tie the game or go for two and win. I talked with Coach Kawal, and we decided to go for the two-point conversion. The play was an option in which I would either keep the ball or flip it to Night Train. When I started to the right, the defensive end crashed, and I flipped the ball to "Train" and he got inside the pylon for the two-point conversion. There was so much noise from the fans who had remained in the stands that those who were departing started to run back into the stadium, but they had missed the best part of the game. We had finally beaten WIU 32-31, and we did it in a very exciting and dramatic fashion.

Two weeks later, our team had a similar situation against Eastern Illinois University (EIU). In this game, I had been sidelined with a knee injury. With three minutes remaining in the game, and SIU behind, I came off the bench and threw a 65-yard touchdown pass to Night Train to win yet another game. My final year of football had been exciting and rewarding. I had the distinct pleasure of playing with some outstanding football players, four of whom went into the pro ranks—Amos Bullocks, Houston Antwine, Carver Shannon, and Marion Rushing.

I must mention a special recognition that the 1958 football team received, specifically my pass to Night Train in the WIU game. Southern Illinois University built a new football stadium in 2009, replacing McAndrew Stadium where games had been played for the past 73 years. During that 2009 season, the Athletic Department had a vote on which was the most exciting moment in the history of McAndrew Stadium. Fans from all over the U.S. were able to cast their votes via the Internet. During the final regular-season game at the Stadium, it was announced that the most memorable moment in McAndrew Stadium history was my last second pass to Lane "Night Train" Jenkins in 1958. This was truly a tribute to the entire team.

However, in the midst of all this, a professor gave me a lesson in priorities. My classwork was going well, and I was completing all of the required courses for a major in chemistry and a minor in math. Dr. Van Lente was my physical chemistry professor, but we also had a friendly relationship outside the classroom, and I respectfully called him "Doc." Dr. Van Lente's son was a big football fan and enjoyed hanging around the team. I gave him my autograph a couple of times, and he looked up to me as a hero. Doc and I were planning a bird-hunting trip when the football season was over. In the middle of the football season, Doc called me into his office to inform me I had "blown" my first physical chemistry exam. He looked me straight in the eye and said, "Bill, you know I will flunk you if you don't do better." I told him I understood. He immediately continued the conversation by asking about the team and other football events. I really appreciated Doc being straightforward with me and reminding me that I had to take care of the business of education first.

The Thrill of Flying

The military side of my senior year was great. I had been promoted to Cadet Lieutenant Colonel, was Deputy Wing Commander, and occupied an important role in keeping the AFROTC unit running smoothly. I was fortunate to meet many distinguished and high-ranking officers in the Air Force. When in the military, it is always an advantage for your superiors to know your name in a positive way.

The last quarter was very important as I would finally begin my flight training. Because I was going into pilot training in the Air Force after graduation, the government paid for 36 hours of flight training. I was thoroughly looking forward to getting into the sky and flying. A friend, who happened to be African American, had gone into flight training the previous year. He told me he hoped I would not get an instructor named Glenn Schuetz because he was prejudiced. One thing I have learned is not to let someone else determine how I should interact with another human being. As luck would have it, Glenn was my instructor. I soon discovered he was not prejudiced, but he was very demanding. I say this respectfully. Glenn "held our feet to the fire" because he wanted us to be outstanding, competent, well-trained, and safe pilots. He did not accept a second-rate performance from any of his students. I soon developed a plan for studying my flight training, and I continued to employ the plan throughout my flying career. When a flight was over, I would go to the dorm, and immediately review what I had done well and what I had done poorly. So, over the different flight-training sessions, I developed a journal about how I had flown the previous days. Before the next flight, I would review these notes and practice my procedures. One day, Glenn said to me, "Bill, you are progressing quite well, and you do not seem to make the same mistake over and over as some of the other student pilots do." Initially, I did not tell him about my system of studying, but I believe this regimen made all the difference in my learning quickly. Near completion of my training, I told Glenn about the book and my system of studying, and he was impressed, to say the least. I gave the book to Glenn, and he shared it with other students for several years.

I think any aviator will agree that the most exciting time in flight training is the first solo flight. This is the time when the instructor gets out of the airplane, and the aspiring pilot must make three trips around the traffic pattern, make three landings, and park the plane. I still remember each detail of that momentous event. Now, all instructors have their special way of saying you are going solo. Glenn and I were flying, and after a couple of satisfactory landings, we were at the departure end of runway two-four at the Carbondale Airport. Glenn looked at me and said, "If you're going to kill yourself, do it alone." He got out of the plane, closed the door, and walked away. This was my signal that I could solo. Most new trainees normally solo after 8 to 13 hours of dual instruction. But on this day, I soloed after five and a half hours of dual instruction. In fact, I think this is still the record for going solo at SIU.

The remainder of my flight training went as well as the beginning. Although Glenn was no-nonsense and exacting, flying with him was fun. I credit him with being the taskmaster that made me a good pilot. I took a two-hour check ride for my license with 31 hours of flying time and received my private pilot's license. I had three hours of flying time remaining that could be used as I wished. Since I wanted to show off my newly-acquired skills, I invited Molly and my friend Charlie Steptoe to fly to Centralia with me. I wanted everyone in my hometown to see that I was a licensed pilot. I also took a couple of my friends and family up for a short ride.

During my training, I did not have any night flying before I got my license. It was getting a little dark, and I was flying the Cessna 172 back to Carbondale. I had never flown at night, so I did not know where the switch was for the landing lights. Now, keep in mind, pilots never admit that they are lost or not sure of what is happening. When we arrived at the Carbondale airport, it was dark. The lights for runway two-four were on, but I did not find the light switch for the airplane's landing lights until I was about three miles from touchdown. I could have landed safely without the landing lights because the runway lights were bright. But, having learned to be calm through football and flying, my passengers did not realize I could not find the light switch.

From Friendship to Romance

Being able to fly with my newly-acquired pilot's license was a great day in my life, and I was happy to share it with Molly because our relationship had blossomed, and we had become "an item" on campus.

After meeting Molly and getting to know her better, I realized she had grown up in a very sheltered and protected environment. She had graduated from high school and was in college at age sixteen, and she had only been on one date before she entered college. I was 21 when we met, and since I thought myself worldly, I became her self-appointed protector. During her freshman year (my junior year) we were living in student dormitories at Thompson Point on the SIU campus. Males and females stayed in separate dorms, but the focal point was the dining room and social area, where students ate, studied, danced, and visited. Although we were dating others, Molly and I had most of our meals together, and we socialized almost daily at the Thompson Point social center.

Molly lived in Villa Ridge, Illinois, a small town 60 miles south of Carbondale. I went to meet her parents and relatives who lived in the area. They were all warm, receptive, and very kind. Molly also visited my hometown, and my two young nieces, Bobbie and Bonnie, took a genuine liking to my girlfriend.

I remember we had Sunday dinner at my home, and Molly was nervous. Now, fried chicken was always on the menu for Sunday dinner, and my mom cooked the best fried chicken I have ever eaten. I embarrassed Molly at dinner because I had eaten several pieces of chicken and put the bones on her plate to indicate she had eaten a lot. She let me know this was not the proper thing to do if our friendship was to continue.

I bought a 1949, two-door, stick-shift Chevrolet. The major problem with the car was that the gearshift would pop out of third gear while the car was moving. Sometimes, while cruising along, all of a sudden the gear would shift into neutral, and I would have to shift it back into third. When Molly was a passenger, her job was to hold the gearshift in third gear while I was driving. At least we had four-wheel transportation and a lifelong romance.

During my senior year we were spending a lot of time together and dating steadily. By the time I graduated, we were "joined at the hip."

Commencement: Excitement, Pride, Reflection and Gratitude

Commencement was an exciting day, to say the least. Although I knew this day was coming, I was not prepared for how emotional I would be. Ralph Waldo Emerson is credited with saying, "Life is a journey, not a destination." Philosophically, I agree, and my graduation was just one of many destinations along my life's journey. However, I was truly humbled when I saw all my supporters proudly attending my graduation. My mom, dad, siblings, and other relatives were glowing with pride. Molly and several members of her family were also present and proud of my success.

When I graduated, I was commissioned into the Air Force as a Second Lieutenant Reserve Officer. I had worked hard during my junior and senior years, and, because of that, upon graduation I was a distinguished military graduate. This might not seem important to some people, and, at the time, it did not even seem like a big deal to me.

However, when I entered the Air Force, I did not go in as a reserve officer, but as a regular officer. The importance of this distinction is that when the Air Force has a reduction in force, the reserve officers are released first. Regular officers have status similar to that of the graduates of the military academies.

During graduation, I thought of my dreams of going to college and playing football. I looked at the reality of those lofty goals and was spellbound and stupefied. Finishing college in four years, majoring in chemistry, having a successful football career, getting a private pilot's license, and graduating as a distinguished military graduate in the United States Air Force—what more could a man want? I was truly blessed.

SIU Photo

Bill in chemistry lab at SIUC.

SIU Photo

Bill at football practice at SIUC

PART THREE

Military and Marriage

"The future belongs to those who believe in the beauty of their dreams."

—Eleanor Roosevelt

With graduation over, I had one month to wrap up loose ends in Centralia, visit Molly a couple of times, and prepare to begin flight school. I hated to leave Molly, but she was still a student, and we both wanted her to complete her studies. Upon departing, when I thought about the future, a mate, and a family, I knew Molly was the perfect partner with whom I wanted to go forward into the future.

I reported to Lackland Air Force Base, San Antonio, Texas, in July, 1959, to begin my initial processing for flight training. Each day was a rapidly, ever-changing situation with orientation, indoctrination, instruction, and physicals. The physicals went well, and I was cleared for flight training. The competitive physical activities were pretty much a snap for me. I was still in good shape and eager to show my fellow aspiring pilots that I was qualified for the flight-training program. I remember one competition that required us to run around barrels spaced 50 yards apart. This race was 200 yards and was run with two people challenging each other. I was matched against an All-American football player from the University of Oklahoma. Fortunately, I beat him and, of course, stuck my chest way out. My fellow classmates also recognized this feat, and I was immediately elevated as a good "jock" in their opinions.

During the third week, I was told that my flight training would be at Moore Air Base, in southeastern Texas. When one gets assigned to a base, there is usually some history about the base. The flight surgeon at Lackland, who was African American, told me that Moore Air Base had never graduated an African American pilot out of primary flight-instruction class. He said he could arrange for me to go to another base. I suppose this is another time the infamous stubborn streak came out in me. I thanked him for the advice and said I would go to Moore and graduate. So, the next week I was off to Moore Air Base in Mission, Texas.

At Moore, pilots were assigned to different instructors who had two to four students. My instructor, Mr. Leary, was the spitting image of my flight instructor at Southern Illinois University. They both were bachelors and neither of them smiled easily. Mr. Leary was also a tough taskmaster. Moore Air Base was a military airbase, but the actual instruction was given by contracted civilians supervised by the military.

The first thing we were told in our initial indoctrination to flight school was to look to our left, look to our right, and one out of the three would not graduate from this primary flight program. The Air Force only needed a certain number of pilots, and the number in training far exceeded the number needed. This proclamation made most of the new officers a bit nervous. So I looked to the left, looked to the right, and said silently to myself, one of you will not make the grade because I plan to graduate. After this briefing, I was off to begin my aviation career in the United States Air Force.

The schedule was set for us to fly in the morning and have classes in the afternoon, or the reverse. We were on the flight line at 0630. We would fly until about noon, go to the classroom until about 1600, and then do our physical training. This flight training consisted of flying 30 hours in a Beech T-34. I had two tablemates, and I got off to an excellent start, soloed early, and was very comfortable with my progress.

The next training was in the T-28 for 115 hours of flying. On my first flight in the T-28, the instructor explained that I should return to the airport and land if the engine sounded rough. Well, on this first flight, when I pulled the throttle that controlled the engine power back to idle, the plane sounded rough as if it might stop at any minute. I asked Mr. Leary if it sounded rough to him, and he said no. He said it was pretty normal, and if there was a real problem with the pistons or rings in the engine shedding metal, a little red light, called a chip-detector light, would turn bright red. Then, it would be time to land and have maintenance check it out. I was glad to hear this explanation because the T-28 certainly had a sound I had not heard before.

In all flight training, having regular, periodic "check rides" are considered normal procedure. I had many check rides at different phases of this training and things were going quite smoothly.

After about 60 hours in the T-28, it was time for another critical check ride. I went to the office where the check pilot would meet me. I arrived 20 minutes early, spit-shined, in a neat uniform, and eager to proceed. While I was waiting for the check pilot, a young woman who worked in the administrative offices greeted me, and we started to talk. She asked who was giving me a check ride, and I said I did not know. After we chatted for about five minutes, the check pilot came in and I jumped to attention and saluted. He told me to sit down and went into his office. He was Lt. Archie Belvin. The young lady said not to worry about my check ride, and she explained further that Lt. Belvin was not difficult but that he liked to give a simulated forced landing at the most inopportune time.

All the check pilots had nicknames or call signs, and Lt. Belvin's sign was "Honcho Thirteen." He was a very imposing figure, and his presence made one's knees knock. Of the last 14 pilots he had given check rides, he flunked 13, and they were all white. In fact, Lt. Belvin told one student pilot he had a "down" as they settled into the cockpit before takeoff. This meant he had flunked. The student pilot asked, "How can I have a down when I have not even started the engine?" Lt. Belvin had him look at the nose wheel. It was still chained to the ramp. Now, that demonstrated a real fear of a check ride or of the check pilot.

Why Did You Come to This Base?

"Honcho Thirteen" told me to preflight the airplane. We got in the T-28, taxied out, and took off. About 400 feet above the ground, he pulled the engine throttle to idle and said, "You have lost the engine." I immediately said I would begin the restart procedures. He said that was unnecessary, because the engine was not going to restart. I explained that I had a field picked out off the left wing for my emergency landing. I made my turn from base leg to final, and it was obvious I would have made the field.

We completed the flight and went back to his office. He had not said anything to me about the flight, and I had no idea what he was thinking or going to do. He closed the door, nodded for me to be seated, and his first words were, "Where are you from?" I replied, "Illinois, Sir." He said he was from Missouri and asked if I knew Missouri was a southern state. I said I thought Missouri was a border state, but he emphatically said it was a southern state. Then he asked, "Why did you come to this particular base for your training?" I said I was assigned to this base. He asked if I had heard anything about this base, and I naïvely said, "No sir." He pursued the interrogation and asked if I had heard that no Negro or colored person had ever graduated from Moore. I lied and said I had not.

Until this time, he had not said whether I flunked or passed my check ride. He finally said to me that it was an excellent flight and that I obviously had been studying and working hard. Then, he very succinctly said, "The only way they can wash you out of this program is to come through me, and since I am the chief check pilot, I do not plan to flunk you." He went on to say my flying skills were outstanding and that I should continue to study and everything would go well. This did two things for me. One, it let me know I had a great chance of completing the program successfully. Second, his confidence in me made me study even harder to be a good pilot. I left his office very happy and went on to graduate from my primary flight training at Moore AB with an excellent record.

Selma: A Shiny New Bird and Encountering the Klan

By March 1960, I had completed primary flight training and had a month off before reporting to basic flight training and my next base. I visited my family in Centralia and spent most of my time with Molly who was still a student at SIU. We had grown much closer during our six months apart. We began to talk about getting married and started to make plans for the future. While in flight training, I did not date anyone, wrote Molly often, and thought about our future even more.

Of course, the time went rapidly, and it was soon time to leave for my next assignment—Craig Air Force Base in Selma, Alabama.

Alabama was the second southern state in which I spent any length of time. When I checked into the base, it was obvious there would be different rules concerning my activity and freedom of movement. I went off base to find the African American community and get a lay of the land from the locals. I was soon informed what was acceptable and what was not allowed because of local customs and laws. I discovered the restaurants available to me and where to attend church. The local population was very impressed with my being an officer in flight school at Craig Air Force Base. This was the first time I was treated like a celebrity just because I was a student pilot.

Basic flight training was similar to the primary training in Texas. My instructor had three students: one Caucasian, one student from Germany, and me. The white student was a few months senior to me and was continually "brown-nosing" the instructor. The German student, Hans, already had 700 hours of flight time. Both were friendly with me, and we had no problems working together. We trained in the Lockheed T-33 jet referred to as the T-Bird, the same type aircraft from summer camp. I was excited and eager to get started with this beautiful, shiny new bird. The typical day in basic training was similar to the previous training regimens. We either flew in the morning, with classes in the afternoon followed by physical training, or flew in the afternoon with academics in the morning.

My first ride in the T-Bird with my instructor was a real thrill. This jet, with tandem seating and wing-tip fuel tanks, was a lot smoother on control inputs than the first two trainers at my primary base. The difference between flying in this jet and training in the other two planes was like night and day. To me, it was like driving my old Chevy or driving my friend's new Thunderbird. The airplane was quiet and seemed to slip through the air more easily than the others. The jet engine was less complicated than the reciprocating engine. There is an expression, "When flying a jet, all you have to do is kick the tires and light the fire." Now, I could say I was training to be a jet fighter pilot, and just the thought of it was exhilarating and made me feel important.

My new base was a military base. The Wing Commander, Squadron Commander, Flight Commander, and all the instructors were military. The support people who worked on the aircraft and other facilities also were military. A unique thing about this base was the number of exchange officers as part of the training command, including six German pilots. The Flight Commander for our section was a British officer, Flight Leftenant Dick. He was British in every aspect of the movie image—tall, thin, and walked with a military strut. He had flown formation in the prestigious Treble One Acrobatic Team in Great Britain. Now, when we think of formation flying and the demonstration teams like the Thunderbirds or Blue Angels, we immediately picture four, five, or six plane formations performing aerobatics. The Treble One flew at times in a 22-ship formation. When we aspiring pilots learned our Flight Commander was one of the leaders of this elite team, we were very impressed. Everything pertaining to our flight training went through Leftenant Dick who was a gentle and pleasant man. He was always relaxed with a smile on his face, very encouraging to the new aspirants, and helpful in every way possible. He was a role model each of us respected, and all the students were excited for the opportunity to fly with him.

I began my flying in the T-Bird and took to it like a duck to water. I was having fun and soloed early. My fellow flight students were encouraging and helpful as we were all working toward the same goal.

Years have diminished my memory of some of the things that happened during this six-month period of training, but a few memorable incidents still stand out. Being one of two African American officers on the entire base was a novelty. The other black officer, a captain, was in administration and had nothing to do with me or any of the pilots in training. Many officers who were training at the same time were supportive and we met regularly to talk about flying.

I often noticed one of my classmates staring at me. Sometimes I would see him peeking around the corner when I would go to fly. One day he came to me and asked if I ever noticed his watching me. I said no because I didn't know where we were going. He explained that he was raised in South Carolina and that the only "colored" people he had been around were in a service capacity. He had never seen a black person in any technical situations. Like many whites, he believed African Americans did not possess the requisite skills to handle complicated machines, especially flying airplanes—even after being proven wrong by the Tuskegee Airmen. He told me he had watched me in academics, in athletics, and in taking off and landing the aircraft. I asked him exactly what he meant. He stated that knowing and seeing me in action had helped him realize that stories about the minimal abilities of blacks were myths and not true. He thanked me for helping him expand his horizons. We became friends. He retired as a three-star general in the Strategic Air Command, and we still keep in contact.

Because I was the sole representative of my race, it caused other instructors and pilots to examine me, fly with me, and watch firsthand how my training was progressing. Consequently, I was afforded the distinct opportunity of flying with several high-ranking officers in the Air Training Command. The positive part of this was that I performed well on these flights, which gave me some "chips in the game" when it came to being evaluated by my assigned flight instructor and the upper-echelon check pilots. Some of the "muckety-mucks" I flew with did not have enough experience in the T-33 to evaluate me under current standards.

However, after being selected, I was able to fly with Leftenant Dick several times. He was notably the best pilot on the base, and he thought I was an excellent pilot. His positive evaluation insulated me from unnecessary and unfair criticism. I recall one flight that I had with Leftenant Dick. As the trainee, I was in the front seat of this tandem-seated aircraft and Leftenant Dick was in the back. After we had flown for about an hour, he asked me to let him fly the plane because he wanted to check the clouds in the area to determine whether solo students would be able to fly that afternoon. He took control of the plane, pulled it almost vertical, and in a calm and smooth manner said the cloud bases were 3,500 feet. We climbed to 11,000 feet with the airspeed slowing all the time. When we reached an altitude of 11,500 feet, he banked the aircraft to the left to start a descent. The airspeed was decaying throughout this maneuver, and when the heading changed to about 30°, the airspeed indicator read zero. I saw him smile as the corner of his eyes wrinkled. I had never seen an airspeed indicator go to zero and the airplane not stall. Normally, when an airplane such as the T-Bird was clean, meaning no flaps or gear were extended, it would stall and lose altitude at about 120 miles an hour. I repeat, as we began to descend, the airspeed at the 30° heading change went to zero. Now, I was amazingly intrigued with this impressive maneuver as I had never seen it before, or since, in my flying career. He smiled in his classic way and said he learned how to do that maneuver in Treble One.

When I started flying solo in the T-Bird and climbing to altitudes between 20,000 and 40,000 feet around cloud buildups, it made me think about the wonder and pleasure a flying career could provide. After flying with Leftenant Dick and observing his incredible flying skills, I thought about one of my favorite poems. Most aviators identify earnestly with this poem. It certainly deepened and strengthened my relationship with God.

High Flight

By James Magee, Jr. of the Royal Canadian Air Force

Oh I have slipped the surly bounds of earth
And danced the skies of laughter silvered wings
Sunward I've climbed and joined the tumbling mirth
Of sun split clouds and done a hundred things
Oh you have never dreamed of, soared, or wheeled or swung
High in the sunlit silence hovering there
I've chased the shouting wind along and flung
My eager craft through footless halls of air
Up, up, the long delirious burning blue
I've topped the snow-capped heights with easy grace
Where never lark or even eagle flew
And while with silent lifting mind I've trod
The high untrespassed sanctity of space
Put out my hand touched the face of GOD!

The universal habit of pilots in flight training was to buy a car. Most of the young officers bought flashy cars, and many were convertibles. I bought a 1957, bright yellow, Oldsmobile 98. The only problem was this car came from the Biloxi, Mississippi area and had been exposed to salt water. A couple of years later, I learned that the salt water had caused rust in the lower panel of my car. I would not let anyone else wash the car, and when I got to the rust spot, I treated it gingerly. When I traded the car several years later, the rust had caused a hole about the size of a grapefruit.

A scary and terrifying incident I experienced in Selma was seeing the Ku Klux Klan. Local residents told me the Klan occasionally made their presence known, and they met in the basement of City Hall, where the police station was also located. The locals believed the Klan just wanted to demonstrate their power to gather members and display their heritage. Now, most of you might remember seeing pictures of the Edmund Pettus Bridge and Broad Street in Selma. Broad Street was six lanes wide, three in each direction, and was pictured in the civil rights march from Montgomery to Selma.

It was a cool evening, and I was driving down Broad Street going back to the base. I was in the middle lane and had stopped at a red light when I noticed something odd about a couple of cars coming behind me in the left lane. As they got closer, I saw a cross on top of each of the cars with incandescent lights to illuminate them. I froze. Locals said the Klan had not harmed anyone recently and were mainly showing defiance and prowess. As they passed, I looked at the cars with my peripheral vision and recognized the pointed "dunce" hat and white robes. The traffic light was still red when they came beside my car. They continued through the red light without slowing down and made a left turn at the base of the bridge into the parking lot at the City Hall and police station. When the light turned green, I slowly drove away and made sure to stay below the speed limit. I prayed I would get across the bridge and to the gates of the base. I was very relieved when I got on base and into the protective arms of the Air Force, but, still, this was an extremely frightening incident. In situations such as this, it is important to balance one's rage with common sense.

Our Wedding in Birmingham, Then Back to the Base

Molly and I were married on Saturday, June 18, 1960, in Birmingham, Alabama. Molly, her mother, Molly's brother Gene, my mom, and my sister Delores drove from southern Illinois to Birmingham. I drove there from Selma. The ceremony took place at St. John African Methodist Episcopal Church with Rev. C. E. Thomas officiating. It was a brief, lovely ceremony, and my bride looked beautiful. I had to be back at flight training early Monday morning, and Molly had to get back for summer school at SIU. Our one-night honeymoon was at the A. G. Gaston motel in Birmingham.

I continued to fly advanced maneuvers, simulated forced landings, and other emergency procedures, and then I began formation flying with two or three airplanes. One day, my instructor was in the airplane with me, and Hans was in the second airplane as my wingman. In formation flying, we were taught that the wingman does exactly as the lead plane. In other words, as the wingman, you must stay closely tucked to the lead plane. Everything was going well on the flight as we flew around clouds with my wingman in very tight. As the lead pilot, I went through a wispy cloud. We had been told not to fly through clouds during formation, but this cloud was so thin I could see all the way through it, and my only other option was to make a really steep dive or a rapid turn which would put my wingman in an awkward position.

When we landed and went into the debriefing, my instructor gave me a down or pink slip, which meant I failed that particular ride. This was the first down I had received on any flight since I began flight training at SIUC. The instructor said he gave me the pink slip because I flew through a cloud. I tried to explain the circumstances, but he did not change his mind. He also gave my wingman a pink slip because he followed me through the cloud. I challenged him on giving my wingman a down, because the wingman is supposed to stay on the lead's wing unless an unsafe flight situation occurs. When I saw the assistant flight commander, I explained the situation to him, and he told me not to worry because everyone gets a down in their flying career. I was not a happy camper.

I began to have less and less respect for my instructor. Not only did he have less experience than my previous instructors, he was not always the fairest individual. On several flights, he would give Hans and me a fair score, and the other tablemate would get good or excellent on similar training flights. However, when Hans and I received check rides with someone else other than our instructor, we would get good and excellent on each maneuver.

The next incident happened while flying at night. Everything was going well, so I thought. When I landed and taxied the airplane to the ramp, I asked my instructor to secure the back seat so I could continue for my solo ride. He told me I would not be going solo because I had not flown well on the dual ride. He explained my airspeed in the base leg turn was four knots slower than the manual recommended. This was definitely a subjective call, since other pilots had five- to ten-knot discrepancies in their base turn and were allowed to complete their solo night flying. When he told me I was not going to fly solo, I was extremely upset and went into the flight shack. Flight Commander Leftenant Dick asked me why I was not flying solo. I explained the situation, and he agreed the airspeed discrepancy was not an egregious error. Leftenant Dick told me to go home and get a good night's sleep. Since the second half of the class was flying the next night, Leftenant Dick instructed me to come the next night so I would not have to fly with my instructor, and I would be able to fly solo.

The next night when I arrived for my flight, the Assistant Flight Commander who was scheduled to fly with me was ill. There was no other instructor to fly with me except my regular instructor. Leftenant Dick told me to fly with him, not to worry, and I would solo. My instructor sheepishly came to me and asked how many gallons of fuel to put in the airplane's fuel tank. I told him the number of gallons required to complete my flight. He asked if we could get extra fuel because he wanted to make a couple of landings. After I had made a couple of smooth-as-silk landings, my instructor took the controls. His landing was horrible. He took the airplane up again, and once more he bounced it while landing. When sitting in the front seat, if something looked untoward or unsafe, the pilot is to take control of the airplane by shaking the aircraft's control stick and saying, "I have it." Since I was not happy with his performance and I was in the front seat, I took the stick, shook it back and forth, and took control of the plane. He then said the engine sounded rough and he heard a noise. There was NO noise. He asked me to land, get another plane, and go solo. That is what I did, and I never flew with that instructor again. I requested that Leftenant Dick be my instructor until my training was complete. My request was granted.

The last couple of weeks of flight training prior to graduation were great. The graduation ceremony was elaborate, and I was sorry that neither Molly nor anyone in my family was able to attend. At graduation, the pinning of flight wings was what each pilot had worked so hard for, and it was the culminating activity. My former instructor had the nerve to ask if he could pin my wings. I specifically told him that, because of the attitude he had shown toward me, there was no way I would allow him to pin my wings. I was honored and pleased when Leftenant Dick pinned my wings. This completed a very successful career in the T-Bird.

For our graduation celebration, our class tried to get the Thunderbirds to perform, but they were not available. Our class then decided to ask Leftenant Dick to fly a demonstration, and he agreed. He removed the wing-tip tanks from the T-Bird and flew one of the most spectacular flights any of us had ever seen. We watched in amazement as he made an inverted pass (upside-down) into a loop and came in and made a touch-and-go landing—a very impressive maneuver. We were excited by his demonstration and pleased that we had chosen him to give us this going-away present.

With graduation complete, we were all anxious about our next assignment.

Throughout our training, we were psychologically indoctrinated to believe that we were second-class pilots if we were not fighter pilots, so most of us aspired to be fighter pilots. The class before us had 60 percent of the assignments for fighter planes. There were 38 pilots in my graduating class, and I ranked number four. I was confident I would be a fighter pilot. As fate would have it, there were only three slots for fighter pilots. Two B-52 slots remained on the board. My tablemate, Dick Maurer, was number five. I looked at him and said, "I guess you are going to Little Rock Air Force Base, because I am taking the B-52 assignment at Travis Air Force Base in California. However, before arriving at Travis, I had to attend classes in weapons, survival, and B-52 training at other bases.

This step ended my basic training at Craig Air Force Base. I was now going to be a B-52 pilot with the United States Air Force. Dreams do come true.

Ten Days of Hell

In September 1960, sporting my new wings, I traveled back to southern Illinois. It was great seeing my bride and the rest of the family. I had a month before my next phase of training, and, as usual, the time sped by like a blur. Molly and I visited relatives and had a brief vacation. Before long, I was on my way to McConnell Air Force Base in Wichita, Kansas, for one week's training in nuclear weapons. This was the beginning of my life in the Strategic Air Command.

The weapons course was intense, with five days of classes jam-packed with new information. While in Wichita, I met an African

American named Rip Gooch, who owned a fixed-base operation at a private airport. He checked me out in several of his airplanes. The one thing I remembered was the difference between flying a Cessna 172 and a Piper Tri-Pacer. The Cessna glided smoothly, and the stubby, heavy, short-winged Piper glided like an anvil. The lesson I learned was that not all airplanes, even those that are similar in size, fly exactly the same.

I had a few days off before I departed for B-52 school, so I went back to Villa Ridge to visit Molly. We were expecting a baby and looking forward to our new addition. Again, time passed quickly, but I was able to get to know my new in-laws and extended family better. These were treasured times, and I began to feel very much a part of the Cross family.

An interim step between nuclear weapons school and B-52 training was a mandatory "survival school." This school was located at Stead Air Force Base about 10 miles northeast of Reno, Nevada. The course was 23 days, from the last part of November until December 20. We were in a very mountainous region, and it was very cold. Our ground and academic training consisted mainly of learning about our enemies, or potential enemies, and how to react to a situation if we ever became prisoners of war.

The first real test was to cross over a field on our stomachs under barbed wire, through holes, and over a big trench. The trench was about 20 feet across and 10 feet deep. The instructors took us out during the day to show us the layout. That night, we were taken to this field and "released" with orders to escape and evade our enemies. The enemy soldiers were Air Force enlisted personnel, and they seemed eager to give the new, young officers a bit of "schooling" about enemy tactics. Of course, we were soon caught and taken to a fenced area representing a prison camp. Eerie and haunting music was played to irritate us in the worst possible way. We were put in an underground, cave-like dwelling and mistreated as badly as legally allowed. One night the "enemy soldiers" brought us out of the cave, stripped us to the waist, and made us do strenuous exercises. After exercising, they pushed us back into the cave. We built a fire to get warm. The fire was a roaring success until one of the guards came in and urinated on it. The resultant smell ran us out of the cave again into the bitter cold.

If you did anything the guards did not like, which could be something as trivial as the way our voices sounded when we spoke, they would put us in a small, box that measured three feet by four feet in which we could not sit or stand up completely. To say this was very uncomfortable would be an understatement of the greatest magnitude. After we were "released" from prison, we began a 10-day trek across the mountains to learn more survival techniques.

This 10-day journey began at an altitude of about 6,000 feet. We wore snowshoes on the snow-covered mountains. Six to seven flight officers were in each group. The rations for this trek were minimal. Each group was given a live rabbit. Each individual airman was given about a pound and a half of beef, two white potatoes, an onion, a small tube of toothpaste, and either two packages of gum, two bars of candy, or one of each.

The first two days of the trek were spent trying to use the unfamiliar snowshoes in the deep snow. The weather was miserable, as it rained, sleeted, snowed, and then rained again. The first night, it took our group two hours to make a fire. What to do with the rabbit became a big decision. Some of the men wanted to make a pet of the rabbit and some did not. For half an hour, we discussed postponing slaughtering the rabbit. I opposed the idea because I could visualize the rabbit escaping. Now remember, I had much experience hunting rabbits, and my mom had prepared rabbit for our meals in a variety of ways. I used my persuasive power to persuade them to allow me to make dinner. I killed, gutted, and boiled the rabbit with a potato and an onion. I think the whole group agreed it was the right decision, and it was the best meal we had during the entire trek.

Our group also tried making beef jerky. This task did not go well, so we boiled the beef with a piece of onion and water and called the mixture stew. Near the end of our exercise, our rations were slim to none. One stick of gum and a bite of candy would be a meal. In my diary to Molly of this experience, I wrote, "Toothpaste never tasted so good for breakfast."

One night on our trek up the mountain, we had to seek shelter outside of our tent. Most of us found a fallen tree with some bare ground beneath it and slipped into our government-supplied sleeping bags. We made a fire and tried to get warm enough until we could get into our sleeping bags and fall asleep. This worked well. However, as I was warming my feet, I got a blister on my toe. Since I only had three nights remaining to complete the trek, I just burst the blister and continued hiking.

On our final night, we had to divide into groups of two or three, escape and evade our enemy, and find our way back to the base. Our group included a Navy pilot, an Air Force navigator, and me. Using our relief map, the Navy pilot and I decided to go about 90 degrees from the direction where we initially started. Then, we made the mistake of listening to the navigator and following his lead for getting back to home base. While we were climbing the mountain, it looked as if it were only about 100 yards until we would cross the peak. Following the leadership of the navigator, we kept going, bit-by-bit, trying to find the peak. We eventually crossed over the top of a 9,000-foot mountain. By this time, we were ready to strangle our leader. We began this trek about 7 o'clock in the evening. Most of the others were at the home base by 10:00 P.M. The three of us arrived at 1:30 A.M. Of course, we refused to talk to the navigator the rest of the time we were at Stead Air Force Base.

When we woke up the next morning, we were very hungry. I had lost 23 pounds during those 10 days. We went to the cafeteria and proceeded to eat everything in sight and drink a gallon of milk. Most of us got as sick as little puppies. This ended survival school, and the next step was B-52 training.

William Ronald Norwood, Junior, and Mastering the B-52

My next assignment was Castle Air Force Base in Merced, California, to begin B-52 training. It was the third week of December, activities at the base were slow, and I was able to take leave. This gave me the first opportunity I had to go back to southern Illinois and see my son, William Ronald Norwood, Junior, who was born December 16, 1960. I was eager to spend time with my family. I flew to Chanute AFB in Rantoul, Ill., and took a train to Cairo. Molly's father, "Daddy George," picked me up at the train station. It was a snowy night, and we had to travel 12 miles to Villa Ridge. I shall not forget this trip. Although he was driving, Daddy George liked to look at me while we were talking. The two-lane highway had many curves and was a bit slippery because of the snow. I was praying, and my heart was in my throat most of the time during the brief, but speedy ride home. Upon arrival, I was very excited and proud to see our son for the first time. We had a big Christmas, with many presents for him—a football, a model airplane, and other toys of absolutely no use to a nine-day-old baby. On New Year's Eve, I headed back to Travis Air Force Base to get into the swing of the training.

The B-52 is a large, eight-engine, jet-bomber aircraft. The crew flying this behemoth consists of six persons: an aircraft commander, the copilot, a radar navigator, a navigator, an electronic countermeasures officer, and a gunner. The first five members of the crew are all officers, and the gunner is an enlisted man, normally the rank of staff sergeant or higher. Each of us flew with different crew members during our training. The training consisted of many maneuvers and operations. From the perspective of the two pilots, we learned to take off and land, fly visual and instrument approaches, practice aerial refueling responsibilities, and assist and command the other crew members. When you are part of a crew, many adjustments are necessary. The first is that you are a part of a team. When a pilot is flying solo, or alone, he or she is the responsible person for everything that happens to the aircraft and any passengers. The crew concept means that the members of the crew must work as a team to accomplish the mission.

This new experience of flying B-52 aircraft was thrilling, challenging, and very different from flying other airplanes. During training we had many long navigation legs. This is not the most exciting part of flying. Most B-52 pilots enjoyed takeoff and landing, low-level flying, in-flight refueling, and the other different aspects that involved flying the "bird" manually. The typical training mission lasted 10 to 14 hours, mostly on auto pilot. On these missions, the actual piloting only lasted about two hours. This was totally different from solo flying when the pilot is flying the airplane for the duration of the flight. This crew idea is a psychological transition for most pilots. After finishing the training at Castle Air Force Base, I was ready to go to Travis Air Force Base and join a permanent crew.

Military "Family Life" and Nuclear Alerts

When I arrived at Travis AFB, in Fairfield, California, I was in for a culture shock. My previous bases had a sparseness of African American officers. At Travis, many African American officers of different ranks, all the way through Colonel, and their families were stationed on the base. This was a large military air transport base. The B-52 and KC-135 refueling squadrons were part of the Strategic Air Command (SAC) and tenants on this base. The sole responsibility of the KC-135 tankers was to refuel the B-52. This meant interactions between the different Air Force units, while at the same time being separate in mission, operations, and orders. Although SAC was a tenant, we had priority on the base when an "alert" was called and we needed to get the bombers airborne expeditiously. Crews stayed in an "alert" compound for three or four consecutive days. This fenced compound had great security. Families could visit, but only from the other side of the fence. While on alert, families were on their own to make decisions. We could only leave the alert facility under a dire family emergency. As a newbie, I was impressed with the food, big color television, pool table, and other amenities. I questioned why those on alert felt so deprived. However, by the third or fourth day, I realized this imprisonment was not a joyful situation. The longer I pulled alert, the more intolerable it became.

Although this was during the Cold War, the B-52 squadron had to be able to get airborne quickly—especially if there were any chance of a nuclear strike being ordered on our enemy, the Soviet Union. This put our unit, although small, in an advantageous position. When we were on alert status, the crews had priority of movement on base. To illuminate my point, if we left the alert compound to go to the movie, we went as a crew. We drove to the theater in a blue, extended-cab truck with lights and sirens. If an alert were called for us to return to our bombers, the theatre lights would come on, a klaxon would sound in the theatre, and the aisles would be cleared. We would run to our truck, turn on our sirens and flashing lights, and all base traffic would stop for us as we sped to our protected aircraft area and prepared to take off.

I was assigned to an excellent permanent crew. We set some records in bombing accuracy on many simulated bomb runs. We were often commended by the Wing Commander and Squadron Commander on our success. After pulling a stint of alert, we would have a couple of days off and then fly a training mission. These missions were normally 14 hours, usually at night, and consisted of a refueling leg, low-level flying, navigation, simulated bomb runs, and a landing. Sometimes we would also practice approaches, takeoffs, and landings.

In June 1961, Molly graduated from SIUC. Two days later, she and Bill Jr. joined me at Travis, and we set up housekeeping for the first time. I finally had my family with me, and that was a happy day. Molly and I knew nothing about married life or living together, particularly on an Air Force base. We started our military career, and I do mean our, because when one is in the military with a family, the entire family is part of the military. We credit our success on getting started correctly to our good friends, Edward and Vertie Young. Ed was a major and had been in the Air Force a few years. He knew the ropes, and his wife Vertie knew the ins and outs of what Air Force officers' wives were expected to do. She helped us in many ways by teaching us military norms, parenting tips, and how to negotiate our way through the Air Force structure. We lived on base and our first home was a one-bedroom duplex. In April 1962, our second son, George Anthony, arrived. George was born on base in the military hospital. We were excited and overjoyed with our new son. We soon moved to a two-bedroom house, and, the following year, we moved into a three-bedroom house.

We regularly attended a non-denominational Protestant church on base. It was always a good service, but the singing was different from what I was accustomed to. One Sunday, the congregation began singing, in their normal cadence, one of my favorite hymns, Amazing Grace. I was singing it as I had learned in the black Baptist church—a lot slower and with a bit of rhythm. Consequently, the congregation was on the third verse of the hymn as I was just finishing the first verse. Molly was embarrassed and elbowed me to stop me from going overboard and being too loud. She often asked me to just mouth the words as my tone and melody are often off key.

During our time at Travis, we took the boys on several vacations to Disneyland, Yosemite National Park, and San Francisco, and we explored many other sightseeing areas in California. We had both of our moms visit for Christmas one year. In March 1963, Molly's mother, "Mama Ada," came and stayed with the boys while Molly and I went to Hawaii. This was our first real extended vacation as a couple, and it was thoroughly enjoyable.

Summer in Montgomery in a Racial Climate

I spent the summer of 1963 in Squadron Officers' School (SOS) at Maxwell Air Force Base in Montgomery, Alabama. SOS is the first formal educational step toward upward mobility in the United States Air Force. I applied, and was accepted, for this prestigious assignment. More than 900 officers were in the three-month course, including 14 African Americans. All of the African Americans were married, but none brought spouses or families due to the lack of suitable housing. Molly and the boys spent the three months with her parents in Villa Ridge.

My friend and fellow crew member, Fay Lamphear, who happened to be white, drove with me from southern Illinois to Montgomery, Alabama. When we arrived at the Air Force Base, African American officers were taken into separate rooms for orientation. We had a special briefing regarding what we could do and where we could and could not go. We were told we should NOT be seen in the front seat of a car with a white driver. (Thank goodness Fay and I were not seen together while driving to the base.) Also, we should NOT be seen going into the front door of a white person's home. At the same time, the African exchange officers were given special identification and passes that allowed them freedom of movement in Montgomery. Now keep in mind, this was 1963 on an Air Force base in the United States of America. To further show how ridiculous the policies were, one of the African American officers bet us he could ride in the front seat of a commercial bus from Montgomery to Atlanta and back and nothing would be said. Remember, this was 1963 when African Americans were not allowed to sit on a bus in front of a white person in some southern cities. The bet was on, and he proceeded to wrap a turban around his head, pretended he could not speak or understand English, and made the trip with no problem at all—even sitting in the front seat of the bus. It was easy money for him. In addition, the Non-commissioned Officers' Club on base was still segregated until word came from the U.S. Attorney General to cease this practice.

As African American officers, we quickly got the lay of the land and avoided some of the camaraderie and partying at the Officers' Club. Several times, a casual evening at the Club with our white peers would consist of a couple of them having too many drinks and invariably making inappropriate statements or telling racial jokes. We found churches to attend and places where we could go, be relaxed, have a good time, and enjoy ourselves without being on pins and needles.

There was one rare exception to the social interaction between the two races. James Brown, "King of Soul," gave a concert in town, and our supervisor's wife wanted to attend. We contacted the local authorities, and she and her husband were allowed to attend with the African American officers. Our group had front-row, center seats and were treated like celebrities—a real plus.

As I look back at this time, I realize how cowardly we, as African American officers, were. Maybe our actions were a product of the racial climate of our society in the country, or maybe we were trying to survive the second-class treatment because of our families and careers. Thanks to the actions of a group of African American officers some six years later, the racial restrictions ceased.

After successfully finishing SOS, I was elated to get back to my family in California.

The Cuban Missile Crisis and Critical Career Decision

During the 1962 Cuban Missile Crisis, my crew was flying airborne alert sorties. On these flights, we carried loaded nuclear weapons, flew for 24 hours, refueling twice before landing back at Travis. During this time when the U.S. and the Soviet Union were on the brink of war, the number of airborne alert bombers with weapons on board was increased. This was a very serious time, although most of the American people then did not understand this precarious situation, and I doubt that many do now. The Soviet Union finally decided to get its missiles out of Cuba, and that was a happy day for all of us who were carrying weapons.

When I entered the Air Force, I planned to make a career in the military. I hoped to do a good job, have a successful career, and secure my family's well-being. I enjoyed flying, and, since few opportunities existed for African Americans to fly outside the military, I planned to remain in the Air Force for at least 20 years, retire, and live happily ever after.

The Air Force Institute of Technology created opportunities for military personnel to attend different universities to get advanced degrees. I thought this was an excellent opportunity to broaden my horizons and strengthen my military career. I was accepted, at Ohio State University to get a Master's degree in Nuclear Chemistry. The only problem was my squadron commander told the Air Force that, if I transferred, it could wreck the unity of the squadron. Now, this was poppycock, and I knew it, so I just sucked it up and said this was one of those stumbling blocks I would turn into a stepping stone.

On more than one occasion, my friend, Joe Griffin, told me we did not need to spend the rest of our lives in the Air Force. He felt we should get out of the military and start careers in business, teaching, or other areas. I told Joe that, as a poor lad from southern Illinois who had already reached lofty goals, I was satisfied with the Air Force and had no plans of leaving.

By 1964, my career was soaring, and I was flying copilot on the number one crew in the squadron. My aircraft commander allowed me to do some refueling and other tasks required of an aircraft commander. I had over 1,700 hours, but the squadron decided that a minimum of 2,000 hours was needed to upgrade. I asked the squadron commander to just give me a check ride to assess my skills so I could avoid the 14 training sessions normally required for upgrading a copilot. I said if I failed the check ride, I would not ask again to upgrade. He explicitly told me "NO."

Our crew's annual check ride was given by the number two aircraft commander in the squadron. He knew my aircraft commander would pass and asked if I would like to get a check ride? I eagerly said yes, and I was pleased with the opportunity to demonstrate my skills. The flight went exceptionally well as did the difficult task of aerial refueling. At the debriefing, and in front of the wing commander, the check pilot told him how well I had performed on the check ride and recommended that I be upgraded to aircraft commander. The wing commander said, "Put Captain Norwood into the upgrade program." I called the colonel aside, and told him I had chosen to change my career path and shared with him my future plans. I had made a decision to go into the airline industry. The commander said he hated to lose me because I was an "up-and-coming" aircraft commander. Then he congratulated me and said that, if he were younger, he would go the same route.

Leaving the military was not an easy decision. The Air Force provided a reasonably secure environment, and my career was going well. However, Molly and I carefully tried to weigh the advantages and disadvantages of staying in the military or going with the airlines. It was a risky decision simply because of the uncharted territory for African Americans. I chose the airlines because I believed the industry potentially had a brighter future.

Bill at T-33 training at Craig AFB, Selma, Alabama.

Bill proudly sporting his shining new pilot's wings.

Bill as a B-52 crew member.

Molly and Bill at a formal night at Travis AFB, Fairfield, California.

Molly and Bill and their sons George and Bill Jr.

George and Bill Jr.

PART 4

Breaking Through the Barriers

"The air is the only place free from prejudices."

—Bessie Coleman, first African American female pilot

Until this time, no African American pilots had flown for the major passenger-carrying airlines. However, after the Civil Rights Bill of 1964 was passed, the airlines started advertising that they were equal opportunity employers. To most people, this meant the doors were wide open to minorities and women. However, as most of us know, the door was only cracked rather than being fully open.

This Act forbade discrimination based on sex or race in the hiring, probation, promotion, and firing of individuals. The Act simply states: "It is unlawful for an employer to fail or refuse to hire or to discharge any individual, or otherwise discriminate against any individual with respect to his compensation, terms, conditions, or privileges, or employment, because of such individual's race, color, religion, sex, or national origin." *Wikipedia*.

The U.S. Equal Employment Opportunity Commission was created and given power to assist people who had been discriminated against in employment and housing. President Lyndon Baines Johnson ordered executive agencies and federal contractors to "take affirmative action to ensure that applicants are employed and that employees are treated fairly during their employment without regard to race, color, religion, sex, or national origin."

This did not mean that unqualified persons would be hired at the expense of more qualified applicants, as some people said. Although I was qualified, I believe if it had not been for the Civil Rights Act, along with the airlines advertising as an "equal opportunity employer," I would not have applied at an airline and certainly would not have been granted an interview. Keep in mind, the Tuskegee Airmen pilots were a highly-qualified group who, until this time, were not hired by the airlines, and I know some of them applied. This was also true for white females in the Women Air Service Pilots (WASP), who ferried airplanes during World War II.

I applied to American Airlines and United Airlines. United granted me an interview, and I went through the process, including taking the long and difficult Stanine test. This test is normally given in a room to a group of applicants. I wound up getting a private test from a professor at Stanford University. When I finished the test, the professor said he was not supposed to tell me how I had done. However, in confidence, he told me that I aced the test. He asked if I wanted to walk to the parking lot with him. I told him no because I wanted to look around the campus since I had never seen Stanford. I did not want to tell him the truth, which was this "highly-qualified and intelligent" applicant he just complimented had locked his keys in the car.

Once I put my separation papers in to leave the Air Force, 92 days before my requested date, the word soon spread about my leaving. Some of the same people who were saying I was good, not excellent, were now saying I should stay in the Air Force rather than go with the airlines. All kind of promises were being made regarding my advancement in the squadron. Of course, I ignored their advice and promises and continued my pursuit of a job with the airlines.

Before United finalized hiring me and assigning a date for starting class, the company's representatives wanted to observe my family and me in social settings. Molly and I were invited to several dinners in San Francisco with different managers within the United hierarchy. I knew the "game plan." Since I would be the first African American pilot at United, they wanted to see if I had proper social graces to be on the point of the spear. Knowing what they were doing, I chose the most expensive restaurants in the San Francisco area and enjoyed "playing the game." I doubt if every applicant received such royal treatment along with being scrutinized.

The last step in being accepted into a class was the physical exam. United had a tremendously large medical department at the San Francisco airport. The physical was progressing satisfactorily. The doctor then nervously asked if I would go to a hospital for an additional test. I knew what he was seeking, but I played along and asked why I could not finish my physical at this magnificent facility. He hopped from one foot to the other nervously trying to find the right words for an answer. Finally, I bluntly asked if he wanted me to take a "sickle cell" test. (Sickle cell is a form of anemia, in which there aren't enough healthy red blood cells to carry adequate oxygen throughout your body. In the United States, it most commonly affects Blacks and Hispanics.) He sheepishly replied yes. I took the test, and all went well.

I bid the Air Force, Joe and Ann Griffin, and all of our friends at Travis adieu. We had developed many friendships at Travis, and we still maintain some of them. I hold treasured memories of my tenure at

Travis. Molly and the boys went to Villa Ridge and stayed with her parents while I started my career with United Airlines.

I must mention my friend, David Harris, who I believe was the first African American voluntarily hired by a major passenger-carrying airline, American Airlines, in December 1964. I say voluntarily, because Marlon Greene applied to Continental in 1963. He was not hired, took his case to the Supreme Court, won the case several years later, and was given the seniority date of when he first applied. In addition, I knew of August Martin flying cargo for Seaboard World Airlines, and Perry Young, Junior, flying helicopters for New York Airways.

"This Is Your World, Man ..."

I arrived at the United Airlines Training Center in Denver on May 31, 1965. I was ready to begin this exciting venture into the airline industry. My first task was to find lodging. Most of my classmates had no problems finding an apartment in Aurora, Colorado, close to the training center, but when I went to the same housing complex to rent an apartment, all the available units had been rented. I thought to myself, this is Colorado, not Alabama, and this state should be more advanced in civil rights. I was in for a great surprise as Aurora was much different from Denver. Denver had a better open-housing policy, while Aurora was more restrictive. I went to an African American realtor and rented an apartment in the mostly African American section of Denver. This was a fortuitous move, because I immediately met some of the community leaders and members who made me very welcome. It was also an area where I had a choice of several churches to attend, so something that began negatively, and could have been disappointing, turned out to be a blessing. Since no African American pilots had trained at United Airlines, the local community treated me like a celebrity—similar to being at Craig Air Force Base, Alabama. Many of the local community members with whom I became acquainted were very encouraging. One day a man told me an expression I have heard through the years, "This is your world man, and I am only renting space and passing through it."

I began to meet my new classmates. At this time, United, and other airlines, were hiring white males with as little as 185 hours flying time. I had accumulated more than 1,700 hours in the Air Force. We trained in a Douglas DC-6, a passenger aircraft with four reciprocating engines. The aircraft held approximately 65 passengers. Now, several of my classmates had done most of their training in the four-seat, propeller-driven, Cessna 172 and were really impressed with the size of this new airplane. When a classmate asked me, in a condescending manner, what aircraft I had flown, I proceeded to tell him I had flown the B-52 and had 1,400 hours in the jumbo jet. I quickly added that the DC-6 would fit under one wing of the B-52. This got his attention, and the word soon spread that my qualifications were far superior to any of those of my classmates. I had confidence in my abilities and could counter quickly the backhanded comments.

The training consisted of academics, learning United's operations and procedures, and understanding the different systems of the airplane and simulator procedures—particularly the emergencies. The classroom work was easy for me since I had been trained on most aircraft systems during my training in the Air Force. None of the new information was a monumental task to understand or conquer. The simulator training was interesting. Among other things, we covered the airplane's systems, pre- and post-flight procedures, standard operating procedures, and how to handle emergencies during taxi, takeoff, flight, and landing. Written emergency procedures for most airplanes have two sections. The first section is composed of boldfaced items that are to be committed to memory. The second portion is on follow-up or cleanup items to complete the procedure and put everything back into working order. This 13-week training session would sometimes be intense. I recall one of the emergency procedures addressed smoke and/or fire in the cockpit. This procedure had 37 memory steps, some of which happened outside of the cockpit. The airlines later decided that if the problem could not be fixed in the cockpit, or other accessible areas of the aircraft, it should not be part of the emergency procedure. If we had an emergency and lost hydraulic fluid, the landing gear had to be manually cranked down. If this occurred, a pilot would go into the passenger compartment and look through a peep hole to see if the wheels were down and locked.

When we finished this phase of training, we were able to actually fly the airplane. We made several takeoffs and landings—the fun parts of flying. As pilots, our initial position would be second officer or flight engineer. A second officer's main duties are to monitor the different systems of the plane and assist with starting reciprocating aircraft engines. The opportunity to fly the airplane was a thrill and allowed us to see if our fellow trainees were "good sticks." A good stick is a person who flies proficiently and smoothly. A silent hierarchy exists among beginners and multi-rated airmen as who rates as the "best stick" in the outfit. My colleagues often referred to me as a "good stick" because of my smooth landings.

I met many new friends in Denver and became reacquainted with some old ones. One of my old friends was Edward "Eddie" Dwight, an excellent pilot whom I had first met at Travis AFB. In 1962, President Kennedy questioned why no African Americans were in the astronaut program. Eddie made history when he was selected for the flight test program as the prelude to becoming an astronaut. When President Kennedy was assassinated, Eddie was dismissed from the flight test program. However, his dismissal might have been a blessing in disguise, because he left the Air Force and became a renowned sculptor. In 1982, he was commissioned by the Atlanta Braves to sculpt the bust of Hank Aaron. One of his most recent works is a sculpture of Dr. and Mrs. Martin Luther King, Junior, in Allentown, Pennsylvania. He has over 100 public art commissions, and many of his pieces are displayed in museums in numerous major cities.

Getting Attention: Favorable and Otherwise

During the last few weeks of training, when I was assured I would finish satisfactorily, publicity started to mount. Molly, Bill Jr., and George came to Denver for a weekend. *Ebony* magazine was going to publish a story on my training and movement into the airline ranks. United also sent a public relations representative to assist and guide both *Ebony* and me through this multi-page production. About the same time, the *Denver Post* did a feature article on me in the Sunday section of the newspaper. We were taken to several posh restaurants, and most of the activities included the boys. We had a great time, and the family was excited about being featured in a national magazine.

Many rumors were floating around United Airlines concerning my being hired. One was that, if United hired this "well-qualified, intelligent, and competitive African American," 20 or 30 of the captains would resign. I am sure that was the way they affectionately referred to me. I had no concern because I felt their threat to resign was ludicrous. Many were high-school graduates, flying captain, with all the attention and accolades the position provided. How could they resign being a captain and go into the competitive world, make the same money, or have a similar position? It did not make any sense that a person who was riding on the top of the occupational skill would do something so dumb. A United representative told me I could not afford to tie my shoes the wrong way. He further explained that some people in United and the pilot group would be looking at United's "Jackie Robinson" and would try to find the smallest detail, hoping I would fail. This made Molly nervous and concerned. I reassured her I would continue to work hard, be proficient, and would welcome anyone to look over my shoulder to try to find something wrong. I think this relaxed her a bit since we had been in these situations several times in the past.

After United had a graduation ceremony and dinner to welcome the new class of second officers into the pilot corps, I left Denver and went to O'Hare International Airport in Chicago to start my flying career and the mandatory probationary period of 12 months.

I arrived at O'Hare Airport and began flying as a second officer on the DC-6 and was lucky to be assigned Captain Don Toeppen as my initial flight manager. Don was an excellent pilot, a gentleman, fair, and a top-notch manager. He welcomed me with a briefing about O'Hare, and I had the usual period of flight supervision to ensure that I was practicing standard operating procedures. I thanked Don and told him I was ready to get started.

Even though the interest in my arrival at O'Hare for my first flight was minimal, the welcome I received at my destination in Cleveland and the welcoming committee of six African American skycaps will always be a treasured memory. (See the Prologue.)

Some captains did find it necessary to look over my shoulder to see if I were qualified to do my job. This did not happen often to the new hires who were white unless some problem occurred due to their lack of experience or talent. I was able to keep these distractions from interfering with the way I conducted myself and did my job. Although a second officer, the idea of being an airline pilot was thrilling. Only one incident happened during the first few weeks as a United Airlines pilot. I was assigned to a flight departing from Omaha, Nebraska, when a passenger who was boarding looked in the cockpit and asked if I were part of the flight crew. I felt honored to be noticed. However, this passenger then said sarcastically, "I certainly don't want to be on an airplane you are flying." As she turned around to go back into the terminal, I sarcastically replied that she had missed an opportunity to fly with an excellent pilot. I also added that I would receive my pay whether she was on the airplane or not. No other major interruptions or mishaps occurred for the six weeks I flew as a DC-6 crew member.

The lesson one learns early in the airline industry, just as I learned back in the Centralia bowling alley, is that seniority means a lot about working conditions and bidding schedules. Bidding is the process of selecting which flights and days to fly each month, days for vacation, and when to upgrade to a new seat or aircraft. I bid to be a second officer on the Caravelle and was awarded the assignment. The Caravelle was a twin-engine jet similar to the Douglas DC-9. It was made in France and came out about 14 years prior to the DC-9. It held the same number of passengers, flew at the same speed, and was much smoother and easier to fly than the DC-9. This new assignment meant going back to the training center in Denver.

By the time I returned to Denver in November 1965, I was able to stay in the United training hotel, and I received a per diem for meals. Caravelle school was not difficult. The airplane was a jewel to fly, and the second officer did not have as many duties to perform as was the case on the DC-6. The training regimen was straightforward and easy to grasp. At the completion of the training, I received a check ride and an oral exam.

During the check ride, which took place in a simulator, I was tested on my knowledge of normal and emergency procedures by a United check pilot whom I refer to as John. This check pilot also gave me the oral exam. I felt very confident that I knew the procedures, aircraft systems, and other material about the Caravelle. When I went for my check ride, John also was being observed by an FAA-designated examiner. John was being extremely "picky" about many minute, irrelevant details, but I was able to handle them all. The Caravelle had 102 "eyeballs" covering the operating systems on the aircraft. The "eyeballs" were white when operating properly, cross-hatch black and white when unpowered, and black when the system was inoperative. One of the questions John asked was, "Of the 102 eyeballs, name the three that do not have an unpowered position." I identified two of them as the parking brake and the pressurization outflow valve, but I could not remember the third one. He was pleased with himself to tell me the third in front of the FAA examiner. We started the oral exam at 7:30 A.M. About 11:30 A.M., John told me we would continue until 6:00 P.M., return the next morning at 7:30 A.M., and finish about 5:00 P.M. I do not know of any oral exam ever lasting that long. The FAA examiner spoke up and said to John, "I think he knows the airplane well." Then, John said I might be able to finish by noon the next day. The examiner repeated his statement regarding my knowledge of the aircraft. John changed his mind and said maybe I could finish by 8:00 P.M. The examiner repeated his admonition for the third time. John asked the examiner if he were satisfied with my understanding of the airplane and its systems. The FAA examiner said he was more than satisfied. Consequently, my check ride successfully ended at that point without going over every system on the airplane.

An addendum to that examination occurred six months later. I returned to the Training Center with a crew for an annual proficiency check ride. The flying portion went satisfactorily, and we began the oral part. The captain was asked a question, which he answered. The copilot also answered his question, and, then, the United check pilot asked me a question. The FAA examiner who was overseeing this proficiency check was the same one who had overseen John six months earlier. The examiner told the check airman it was not necessary to ask me questions because I knew the airplane extremely well. This was the easiest check ride I had in my career at United, thanks to an observant FAA examiner.

Dealing With Prejudice on the Ground and in the Air

When I arrived at O'Hare in September of 1965, I had to find housing. Molly and the boys were with Molly's family in Villa Ridge. Molly's brother, Virgil Cross, and his wife, Helen, lived in Chicago. They invited me to stay with them while looking for a house, and I took them up on their generous and gracious offer. I guess I was naive, but I did not think finding housing for my family would be a difficult task; nor did I realize how segregated housing was in Chicago and many of its suburbs. I received the assistance of a non-denominational, multiethnic housing alliance. The Chair of this group called a person he knew who managed several buildings in Evanston, Illinois, and was told four apartments were available. One hour later, Molly and I, along with the housing representative, were in the Evanston office eager to look at the apartments. After realizing the new airline pilot, who United Airlines trusted with $2 million worth of aircraft, was the renter, the building manager suddenly remembered that the four apartments had just been rented. Perhaps he noticed the color of my skin.

In December 1965, we did find a townhouse to rent in our price range in Park Forest, Illinois. Park Forest was noted as having an "Integration Maintenance" program for the purpose of avoiding block-busting and white flight from the suburb, while successfully maintaining a well-balanced, integrated village. It was a great community for our young family. Although we lived there only two and a half years, Molly and I were active in the community. Molly taught third grade at Lakewood School, we joined Faith United Protestant Church, and we had wonderful friends and neighbors. If not for the long distance to the airport, we would have bought a house in the community.

I loved flying the Caravelle. This plane held 64 passengers and was easy to fly and land. Often I would fly the "Executive Flight," which traveled from Chicago to Newark once a day at 5:00 P.M. This particular flight was normally all male and all first class, with unlimited food, drinks, and cigars. This was long before the non-smoking rules. Two weeks during December, all passengers on these flights would receive very nice gifts, such as electric shavers, leather goods, and books.

Nothing startling happened during the time I was flying the Caravelle except for a few improper and offensive remarks made by a couple of captains. Keep in mind, I was in my probationary year and could be terminated "just because... ." On several occasions while flying, a captain would tell inappropriate ethnic and/or sexist jokes. I would politely and respectfully explain my dislike for these jokes. I needed to be careful how I voiced my opinions as I did not want to be labeled as a troublemaker or "uppity." Most of the captains respected my opinion, but several did not. I had to "bite my tongue" more than once. However, after I completed my probationary period and became a full-fledged union member, I spoke forcefully against ethnic and sexist slurs and jokes. I left no doubt as to how I felt about this subject. Unfortunately, in the past couple of years, I have received calls from young African American pilots, still in the probationary year, who encountered the same or similar situations. My advice was, "Suck it up until you are finished with your probationary term. Then, handle the situation as you think best."

Other than this problem, the flying during my probationary year was very good. Occasionally, a captain would allow me to move from the second officer seat to the first officer seat and fly a leg.

"I'm Just a Rich Black Man"

During one of the public relations events when I was initially hired with United, I met a vice president of Alitalia Airlines. At the end of a lengthy conversation, he said he would like to give me a trip anywhere in Alitalia's system. I was shocked, surprised, and apprehensive. Molly was overwhelmed with joy and excitement. After we got home, reality kicked in, and I explained to Molly that, even if we had free air travel to Europe, we still had to pay for food and hotels. In the first year and on a second officer's pay, our ability to do this seemed out of the picture. However, Molly was very persuasive, and looking at our budget and savings, off to Italy we went. The boys stayed with Ed and Vertie Young, who were then stationed at Scott Air Force Base in Belleville, Ill. Since this was our first flight out of the country, we had to get passports, traveler's checks, and, of course, new luggage. The trip was amazing, and we visited all the tourist sites in Rome, Pompeii, Naples, and Milan. On one of our bus tours, I was talking with a farmer from Idaho. He was touring Italy for three weeks. I explained that we were there for a week but would probably return next year. He bluntly asked what my occupation was that could allow me that luxury. Before I could respond he said, "You must be an athlete or an entertainer," and suggested several names. I simply replied, "I'm just a rich Black man." I often wondered if he would have been that friendly and talkative if we were back in Idaho.

Our scheduled return flight was from Milan to New York and on to Chicago. When Molly and I arrived in New York, we noticed a flight leaving in about two hours from Kennedy Airport to San Francisco. At the last minute, we decided to go to California and visit our good friends, Joe and Ann Griffin, for a day. We called the Griffins, rechecked our bags, and off we went. The time zone changes soon caught up with us, but we were "jet-setters" for a day. This was the flexibility of travel opportunities years ago.

A Health Scare Rare Enough For a Medical Journal

One interesting and unnerving thing happened during my second year at United. We had one of the largest blizzards in Chicago history on January 26-27, 1967. I had shoveled quite a bit of the 30-plus inches of snow. In February, when I went to take my annual physical at United's Medical Department, my EKG indicated an inverted T-wave. The test was repeated and things did not improve. I was taken off flight status because it appeared I had suffered a mild heart attack. This was disconcerting because I could see my career ending. I was sent to United's heart specialist in Washington, D.C. After many tests, the examining doctor was able to determine a lot about my life, lifestyle, and activities, and he even stated that I probably was a football player. He asked if I had the mumps recently. I said no, but remembered that our son, George, and Molly both had the mumps several months before. The doctor explained that there was nothing wrong with my heart and that I had not shoveled too much snow. The mumps virus had infected the sack around my heart, and that caused the erroneous reading on the EKG. The malady was pericarditis. I was ordered to take it easy, not to fly, and to have periodic EKG's until readings were normal again.

Because this was not a common occurrence, the doctor asked if my case could be written up in a medical journal. I happily agreed since his professionalism saved my career. Don Toeppen, my flight manager, reassuringly told me that he, and United, would do whatever was necessary to keep my family and me with financial resources until I could return to flying. This was a comforting gesture, but, fortunately, it was not necessary. I followed doctor's orders and returned to flying in a month.

I flew the Caravelle for about a year and a half and then upgraded to second officer on the Douglas DC-8. This four-engine airplane had a passenger version and a cargo version. The cargo version had two additional seats in the cockpit. Occasionally, we would fly 30,000 plus pounds of strawberries. During four- to five-hour flights, the smell from the berries became very strong and nauseating. I also remember flying expensive horses on several occasions. The horses' groom would sit in the cockpit and was often smellier than the horses. We also had to stay away from lightning and storms, because such meteorological conditions would agitate the horses, and the groom would have to go back and calm them during the flight. Only in rare cases could passengers get such royal treatment.

In 1968, I upgraded to first officer, or copilot, on the Boeing 720. This was an easy transition for me since the 720 was similar to the B-52. The 720 was a civilian version that was similar to the KC-135 tanker. I flew the airplane well and was pleased with my progress. However, one day I was flying into Portland on a nice, calm, clear, late afternoon. In the landing flare, the airplane sunk quickly, and we landed a bit hard. I had been flying with this captain for two weeks and had "greased" my prior landings. He was shocked, and so was I. The captain asked me to fly the next leg hoping that we could figure out what the problem was. Then, it dawned on me that I had reverted to flying the B-52, which floats well during the landing phase, whereas the 720 did not float as well. My reversion back to an airplane I had flown earlier had caused the problem. I certainly learned each flight is unique, since aircraft, wind conditions, and runways are not always the same.

Finally, a Home in Elk Grove Village and a Turn at Teaching

Molly and I started looking for housing closer to the airport. On Sundays, we would go to different communities to look at model homes in new developments. One disastrous trip was to Hinsdale. After looking at the models, I asked the usual questions, "If we bought, how soon would we be able to move in, how were the schools, how much were taxes, etc." The sales representative could not answer any of the questions. It was hard for me to believe that on one of the busiest days for selling homes, none of this information was available. I asked if he preferred that African Americans not buy in this development. He readily admitted he did not own the property, but it was the developer's policy not to sell to African Americans. I stated that the owner could not exclude us from buying since federal money was involved in the building of these homes. When I noted most of the new homeowners in this area were coming from the Chicago suburbs of Cicero and Berwyn, I knew this would not be the best community for my family. With an office full of gawking people and my being upset and angry about this blatant act of racism, I said in high decibel that we would not buy a house in the development because the families they were attracting were not in our class educationally, financially or socially. The onlookers were so shocked one could hear the proverbial "rat pee on cotton."

In July 1968, we moved into our first home in Elk Grove Village. At this time, many realtors would not show houses in the Northwest suburbs of Chicago to African Americans. However, without any hesitation, the builder Centex readily sold us a house. We were the fifth or sixth African American family in the village, which had an approximate population of 25,000. We had wonderful neighbors and friends in Elk Grove, several of whom still maintain close relationships with us.

Our boys completed elementary and high school in Elk Grove. Both were involved in the Junior High and High School athletic programs. We joined Prince of Peace United Methodist Church, and Molly and I served on several church committees. Molly was elected as a trustee on the Elk Grove Library Board. One of the first people to welcome us to the neighborhood was Bob Haskell, principal of Elk Grove High School. Bob asked me to substitute teach there on my days off from flying, and I agreed to give it a try. The high school had an enrollment of about 2,500 students, with only two African Americans.

My first class assignment was teaching a freshman boy's physical education class. As I was taking attendance, I heard a student say, "Mr.

Jones (the permanent teacher), sure is dark today." When asked about the comment, the student first denied it, but later repeated the statement. I acted as if nothing were wrong. We were playing football, and I assigned the student to a team. I joined the opposing team and played across from him. On the first snap of the football, I "decked" him with a forearm to the chest, and he stumbled backwards. The second play was a repeat of the first. I helped him up, and he apologized. Then I replied, "Mr. Jones may be darker today, but he's also a lot tougher." Upon reflection, I know my actions were inappropriate, and I would not do that today.

After substituting several times, I had developed a good rapport with students and teachers. Because of my background in mathematics, physics, chemistry, and English, I asked to substitute in these classes. Of course students knew when they had a substitute how to prepare, or not prepare, for class. Once, in a chemistry class, I asked a couple of questions, and no one knew the answers. I gave the class 20 minutes to read the lesson and said if anyone could ask a question from that material that I could not answer correctly, I would give her or him a dollar. Needless to say, no dollars were given out, and they met my objective of reading the material.

Often teachers would call to see which days I would be available to substitute for them, giving me a feeling that administrators and teachers respected my teaching and classroom control. One day, two students were pushing and shoving in the rear of the room, and one spat on the other. I hate spitting, and I took them to the office. I suggested that one of the students, who had a reputation for being disrespectful to students and teachers, be suspended, and it was done. The other student, who was currently making C's and D's, had no prior blemish on his record. I suggested he not be suspended if he would study diligently and stop being a pain to the teachers. He agreed, and for the next five semesters his grades improved to A's and B's, and he brought his report card to show me after each grading period. He thanked me for having high expectations of him and giving him a second chance.

After a couple of years of substituting, and with the blessing of the administration, a history teacher, Ms. Dorothy Lewis, and I co-taught an elective class for juniors and seniors—a course about the history of minorities in the United States. Several teachers questioned why such a course was necessary in an "all-white" student body. Our explanation was, "Who better to be exposed to this history?" The class was always full, and the students were excited about learning history that was inclusive of all Americans—including African Americans.

One of the culminating activities in this class each semester was preparation of a "soul food" dinner. I enjoyed this as much as the students, since it gave me an opportunity to "show off" my culinary skills. I thank Bob Haskell for the opportunity he provided me to teach and to learn from students. A couple of years ago, at a golf course in Arizona, I met a young lady who remembered being in one of my classes.

In 1971, there was an oil crisis in the United States. Some pilots were furloughed, and some had to change airplanes and/or positions. I changed aircraft and became the copilot on the Boeing 737. The transition to the 737 went smoothly, and my flying schedule was better.

An MBA and Becoming a Trustee

Because of my medical scare, I wanted to go back to school for an MBA degree. My schedule and seniority on the 737 allowed me to do just that. So, from 1972 to 1974, I went to the University of Chicago and completed my MBA in Industrial Relations. Going back to school was a great experience, but I am mindful of, and thankful for, the sacrifices my family made in order for me to complete this task. Receiving my MBA gave me great comfort, because I knew that I would be better prepared to enter the business world if something happened to my flying career.

In 1974, I was excited and humbled to be appointed to the Southern Illinois University Board of Trustees. Bob O'Daniel, Executive Director of the SIUC Alumni Association, asked if I would be interested in serving as a trustee and submitted my name for consideration by Governor Daniel Walker. When I was appointed by Governor Walker, I did not know much about the role and responsibility of a university trustee, but I was eager to serve my alma mater and its students. I was the first graduate of the University appointed to the Board. During my tenure on the Board, I learned a great deal about the University and how it functions. Being a board member has a steep learning curve if you are only there for a short time. I was first appointed to finish the term of a member who resigned with two and a half years remaining. I was then reappointed by subsequent governors to multiple six-year terms, serving a total of 27 and one-half years.

I had excellent mentors who served on other boards in addition to the SIU Board. I formed some great relationships during my tenure. At this time, the Board consisted of seven members, all appointed by the governor, with no more than four members from any one political party. The board struggled with some issues, agreed and disagreed, and sometimes had 4-3 votes, but I can honestly say, I never felt an issue was politically motivated along party lines.

My philosophy about educational institutions is that they exist for the students. I made it a point to take time to talk with students on all SIU campuses. I could rely on most students to give an honest appraisal of their educational experience and/or instruction. This was particularly true because they did not perceive me to be part of the administration. My interaction with students was informative and helpful in my decision-making process. Since I was an aviator and a former athlete, I was attracted to the aviation and athletic programs. My other commitment was to be present at graduation programs on the campuses at Carbondale and Edwardsville, as well as the medical school in Springfield. I attempted to shake as many graduates' hands as possible when they crossed the platform. After the University started holding graduation ceremonies for each discipline instead of en masse, it was easier to congratulate more students. It would not be unusual for me to attend six to eight commencements over a weekend.

I chaired the SIU Board and was on the Illinois Board of Higher Education (IBHE) for three years. I also served on the Board of Trustees of the State Universities Retirement System (SURS) as an SIU representative for 24 years—20 as treasurer and three as president. This Board supervised the investments and managers of the retirement system for the state universities' pension fund.

Being on the SIU Board was particularly gratifying and rewarding. I will always be grateful for the opportunity to have served the University that did so much for me. Some of the Board members with whom I served are among my closest and dearest friends.

Family Life and Family Fun

Being an airline pilot provided many benefits. Molly and the boys were excited with the travel perks and used them to the greatest extent. One of our favorite destinations was Hawaii, and we vacationed there at least once a year. I remember one flight from Hawaii to Los Angeles when Bill Jr. and I were sitting upstairs in first class on a B-747 playing a card game called "Coon Can." This has often been considered an ethnic game among some African Americans. Actually, the original name was Conquian, and it is generally regarded as the earliest form of Rummy played with a Spanish deck of cards. While we were playing, a very happy and friendly lady approached us and asked about our card game. It was Carol Burnett. We explained our game and had a wonderful visit with her that lasted for at least an hour.

The boys' first flight out of the United States was to Amsterdam, which they enjoyed immensely. It is hard to remember all the vacations we enjoyed, but a few included Florida, California, and the Bahamas. However, many of our vacations were driving trips to Wisconsin and Canada for fishing and snow skiing; to Door County, WI for camping; to Kentucky Lake for boating and water skiing; and many trips to Villa Ridge.

Molly's home in Villa Ridge was an important part of my life, and the impact of our many trips there cannot be overemphasized. The "Cross Compound," on about 100 acres of land in a very rural area, was home to her parents who were fondly called "Mamma Ada" and "Daddy George;" her brother Gene, his wife Merelyn, and their children, Darryl and Gena; and Aunt Florence and Uncle Hugo.

Molly's parents gave us some property on the compound. We built two ponds and spent many happy times fishing for bluegill, catfish, crappie, and bass. It may be difficult to understand the happiness and freedom that being in the country provides, but it was a thrill for all of us and many of our friends.

The boys were both active in high school sports, and watching their games provided hours of fun and excitement. George played football and ran track. Bill Jr. was in basketball, football, and track. They both did well and played on the first teams at their respective levels. A memorable highlight of one football game was when George (quarterback) threw a touchdown pass to Bill Jr. (running back) that was captured on video. The newspaper headlines the next day were, NORWOOD TO NORWOOD. Now, you know I was one proud papa.

The 1980s: New Year's Eve in Hawaii, an Empty Nest

In 1980, I went to the DC-8 as copilot and flew in this position for four years. This was an easy transition as I had flown this plane as second officer. My tenure on the DC-8 was fairly routine with no significant incidents. I was senior enough to hold schedules flying to choice destinations. One of my favorites was flying to Hawaii during the winter months. I remember one trip when I was in Honolulu and due to fly back to Chicago on New Year's Eve as Molly and I planned to go to a party. As Mother Nature would have it, Chicago had a snowstorm and I had to stay in Honolulu an extra day. This allowed me to experience New Year's Eve in Hawaii, and I was kept awake all night by the sound of hundreds of thousands of firecrackers. The next morning, the streets were covered with firecracker residue.

Molly and I were now "empty-nesters" and decided to move to a smaller house. The move took us to Rolling Meadows, just a few miles from Elk Grove, but due to Molly's "house hunting" our new home was a bit larger. Molly had just graduated from Northern Illinois University with a Master's in Education and was now a reading specialist at a local elementary school about two miles from our new home. She later had a publishing and consulting business and served on the Harper Community College Board of Trustees for 11 years.

One of the activities I thoroughly enjoyed was speaking at schools. This began when I first started with United Airlines, but during the 1980s it was not unusual for me to speak at a school once or twice a month—from kindergarten through high school. I was always gratified by some of the questions young people asked. Most of them had a grasp of many occupations, but they had little knowledge of the duties of a professional pilot. This was especially true in the African American communities, where there had not been speakers in that career field. Often, I would get several letters from some of the teachers I visited telling me how important the visit had been to their students.

I visited schools ranging from the most affluent to the most economically-deprived communities. I learned many lessons from these visits and soon realized how important it was to have high expectations of students for their success. Quite simply, if excellence is expected from the attendees, excellence will be aspired to and achieved. Conversely, if low achievement is expected, students will often live down to our minimal, pre-conceived notions. I also learned how important it was to immediately grasp the attention of the young minds, maintain control, hold the attention of the group, and never promise something that could not be delivered. The following two incidents come to mind.

I went to Gary, Indiana, to speak to a group of students, ages 12 through 17. When Molly, our nephew Robyn, and I arrived at this two-story building, there were approximately 300 youngsters in attendance. As I began to speak, one of the young lads toward the rear of the room decided he would add a little fun and made a noise and inappropriate action. I said to the entire assemblage that these actions would not be tolerated. When the young man did it a second time, I walked to the back of the room, told him he was excused, and escorted him out the door with explicit instructions not to return. I went back to the front and successfully finished my talk with the rest of the group. The attention of the remaining students was excellent, questions were appropriate, and comments following the meeting were congratulatory.

Another incident occurred when I spoke at a career day assembly at a Chicago south side high school. Professions were represented by about 30 participants, including my good friend Roland Burris who was Attorney General of Illinois. The school day was to end at 3:30 P.M.; however, the principal suggested we leave about 3:10 P.M. since there had been a shooting the day before. Most of the career representatives agreed with this idea.

The only problem was, I had spoken with several of the senior students and through the conversation was asked about my athletic ability. They asked if I would stay after school and play softball. I had agreed and felt I could not disappoint these young men. So, after school, we went out to the black-topped schoolyard and played softball. When it was my time to bat, I luckily hit a ball over the fence. The young men were very impressed with this "old man" who they said still "had his stuff together." We played ball for about one hour and had a wonderful time. Not once did I have any concern for my safety. Most of the students at this school were outstanding class members and wanted to learn.

I had the pleasure of accompanying United's CEO, Stephen Wolf, to several schools in Chicago. I mention this because he was not only willing to go into the inner-city schools, he was relaxed and comfortable in doing so. He spoke of his growing up in a less-than-desirable situation. He also often, and without publicity, quietly invited groups of young people to the United Airlines executive offices, showed them around the operation at the airline, and treated these youth to lunch in the boardroom. I am sure his actions made a difference in many lives.

The Top of the Ladder: Captain

Being a captain is the epitome of an airline pilot's dream. I took a captain's slot at O'Hare and was off to Denver to train on the B-727. After the usual classroom instruction on the aircraft, its systems, emergency procedures, and standard operating procedures, I met my simulator instructor. My first simulator ride went well, and the instructor asked if I had piloted this airplane previously. I had not been on the 727 in any flight capacity, and I had only ridden in the cockpit on a couple of occasions. It would be an understatement to say that the next nine simulator rides were enjoyable. I was ready for my check ride from an FAA examiner, and my instructor assured me I would enjoy this check ride and pass successfully. There were five FAA examiners in Denver; four were outstanding, and one was a jerk. Of course you know which one I was assigned. In fact, when I initially met him, the first thing he asked was what I thought about the air traffic controllers' strike, which was in progress at the time. I told him I had been too busy learning the aircraft to worry about a strike. Actually, I was fully aware of the strike, but a discussion with him about the strike was a no-win situation. We went into the simulator for the first part of the check, and I was confident I had flown the plane well. The examiner said the simulator examination was over, but he wanted me to make one more takeoff in the simulator. I agreed. He had programmed an unflyable wind shear situation, and I eventually crashed. I still remember the smirk on his face as he said, "I just wanted to show you that you are not as good as you think you are, but you did keep it airborne longer than I thought you would." We went for lunch, and, of course, everyone at the Denver training center knew I was getting a check ride. Several colleagues asked how things were going as they passed our table, and I would innocently shrug. The examiner told everyone who asked that I had done okay in the simulator but that he would "get me" on the oral examination. We began the oral, and I answered all the questions on the systems. When we got into the emergency procedures, he would describe an emergency scenario, and I would give him the immediate action steps and call for the cleanup checklist, as instructed. He told me my reply was unacceptable, and he wanted me to do the entire check list. My copilot, who was also a Denver instructor, explained to the examiner that my answers were correct and "by the book" as taught in the training center. After talking with one of his friends for about 10 minutes about fishing, he reluctantly signed my temporary license, and said he thought I would be okay. I fumed at his attitude but managed to stay calm.

Molly had been waiting for my promotion to captain as much as I had, and first on her list was a big celebration. Since she loves to plan parties, she was thrilled. About 400 family and friends attended a gala event with plenty of food, drinks, and a live band. I think Molly spent my entire raise on this party.

When I became captain, I was pleased and overwhelmed with the attitude of my colleagues. I flew the B-727 about six years and then the B-757 and B-767 for a couple of years. The B-757 was a magnificent airplane, and I enjoyed flying it more than any airplane. I flew the DC-10 for three years until I retired. This jumbo jet, with the feel of the Cessna 172, was fun to fly and easy to land.

Once promoted and earning the pinnacle of an airline career—the position of captain—I was eager to be the best leader possible. The one thing an understudy can do is watch and learn from other captains. Most of the authority figures I flew with were excellent, but a few were poor. As first officer, one looks to the left seat, the Captain's seat, for the final decision. Out of habit, some new captains look to the left when an important decision is necessary and see only reflections of themselves in the windshield. It is also important not to become too enamored with the new celebrity status of most people saying, "Sir." If so, you are soon brought down from the clouds when your spouse tells you to take out the trash.

My leadership philosophy was simple: we were not a separate cockpit crew and cabin crew, but a single unit—one crew. I had seen too many events and circumstances in which the captain could have been more supportive of the flight attendants. I also extended the same respect to the rest of the United team, including mechanics, customer service representatives, cabin cleaners, and others. This attitude served me well, and I developed many lasting relationships throughout United Airlines. I was often asked why flight attendants were so courteous and friendly to me. My answer was that I always tried to treat everyone with respect and value their job and contributions to the goals of a safe, efficient, and pleasant flight.

In 1985, a pleasant surprise awaited me when I arrived in the flight planning operations area for a flight. The other crew members were Jim Edwards, first officer, and Eldridge Johnson, second officer. This happened to be the first time United had an all African American cockpit crew. Fortunately, during our two days of flights, none of the passengers raised eyebrows or had a look of consternation.

Memorable Passengers: a First Class Jerk and a Real Champ

Through the years, Molly has, more than once, heard my stories of unruly passengers and incidents with people on the ground. She suggested I share a few and chose the following.

Have I ever had a person removed from a plane? Unfortunately, the answer is yes. Most of the time, the threat of being removed is enough for an unruly passenger to change her or his behavior. However, on a flight leaving Dulles Airport for Chicago O'Hare, the lead flight attendant informed me that a first-class, premiere, male passenger had become a problem. He had brought three bags aboard, and the flight attendant explained that the baggage compartments were full and that she would have to check one of his bags. His comment to her was, "NO, you are here for service, not safety." He continued to be aggressive and threatening. I went to the passenger and told him he would have to deplane, at which point he said he would, "Be good." Another first-class passenger said this unruly person had used profanity and referred to the flight attendant as a "Gestapo bitch." The attendant was visibly shaken, and after discussing the situation with three flight attendants, I made the decision not to allow this passenger to remain on the plane. I announced to the other passengers there would be a delay due to the removal of a passenger. The flight attendants and I had complete support from the other passengers in first class, and several offered to write in support of my decision in case there were any repercussions because of my decision to remove the passenger. I thanked them but told them it was not necessary because my action was in compliance with FAA regulations and United's standard operating procedures.

I came very close to removing another passenger and his family who had seats in two rows. The father insisted that his 11-year-old son sit next to him by the exit door for takeoff. The flight attendant had explained the FAA regulation that no child under age 16 could occupy an exit row for takeoff and landing. This made no difference to the man, and he refused to move his son. I went back to his seat and informed him that he had 10 seconds to make the move or leave the plane. As he started to argue, I said you have seven seconds. Begrudgingly, he moved his son to another seat.

A disturbing incident happened on a flight leaving Newark. We had backed away from the gate and were taxiing to the runway for takeoff when a passenger started to run down the aisle screaming that he needed to get off the plane. He said he had left his car running in the parking lot. This was very alarming, so we returned to the gate. It was necessary to have all passengers deplane and claim their luggage. We could not take any chances that he had a device in a piece of luggage that would remain on the aircraft. Other than departing late, the flight continued without any additional problem.

After non-smoking rules were established on airplanes, occasionally a passenger would use the bathroom to sneak a smoke. When this happened, I would ask for the police to meet the plane. This is a serious matter because if a fire were accidentally started, it could be disastrous. If the smoke detector in the lavatory is tampered with, it becomes a federal crime, and the punishment is severe. This happened more than once, and although no one was ever arrested, I could always count on the police to make the passenger uncomfortable and miss the next flight if he or she was scheduled to resume traveling.

One of the strangest things happened early in my career on a flight from San Jose, California, to Denver, Colorado. I was flying first officer on the DC-8 with a captain who was new to the plane and also a flight manager. The plane boarded passengers from outside via stairs. About 20 minutes after takeoff, a flight attendant called me in the cockpit with a problem. She asked if I noticed the young lady with multicolored-hair who had boarded the plane. I replied yes. She said the lady had taken a "hooded" rat from her purse. I asked the flight attendant what a "hooded" rat was, and she explained the rat's coloring. She further stated that she had instructed the lady to put it back into her bag, and the passenger complied. The captain wanted no part of this problem, so according to protocol, I called ahead to Denver and asked for a United representative to meet the plane. Upon arrival at the gate, no one in management was present. Frustrated to say the least, I went in the terminal and retrieved a Passenger Service Agent (PSA). I relayed the story to the PSA and ushered the passenger into the terminal. When I saw the PSA a few minutes later, I asked about the disposition of the matter. Since the passenger was not continuing on another flight, the PSA told her, "Good, because you caused the crew some consternation."

I was aghast. I explained if a rat got loose on an airplane, it could eat into electrical wires, the fuel line, and other important parts of the plane, or, worse yet, have babies. The aircraft would be grounded and taken out of service until it could be thoroughly inspected and searched. Imagine sitting next to a person who pulls out a rat; someone might have a heart attack. Disgusted, I stated if the situation ever happened again, I would land the plane at the closest airport—even if it were in Winnemucca, Nevada—and the company could come there and take care of the situation.

Unruly passengers were definitely in the minority. Most people were thankful to reach their destination safely. I have met many celebrities, some who were just getting started in their careers and now have private jets. The nicest, most humble was Muhammed Ali. In the boarding area, he would take time and sign autographs, talk with other passengers especially if children were present. I had several opportunities to meet and visit with him. He loved to be called "Champ." When I would speak to him, he would always greet me saying, "Hey good buddy, how are you doing?" This would open the conversation, and we would sit and visit for a while. He always appeared very interested in our conversation and never seemed to be in a hurry.

Fueling a Fight

Oklahoma City, 1987, provided an opportunity that slapped me—a "hotshot" captain—back into reality. We had been at the airport for 50 minutes, and our plane was the only United airplane on the ground. About 10 minutes before starting the engines for departure, I noticed that the fuel on the airplane was 100 pounds short of the dispatch amount. I requested more fuel. The young, white male who was dispensing the jet fuel came into the cockpit of the B-727 and asked the white second officer if he were going to delay a flight for only 15 gallons of fuel. I turned to the lad and reminded him that, as captain, it was my decision, and not the second officer's. He sarcastically repeated the query to me, and I responded, "If 100 pounds is 15 gallons, then put it on the aircraft, and give me a new fuel sheet." In an unacceptable tone of voice, he told me a new fuel sheet was not required. I immediately replied, and, in very specific terms, stated "If a captain asks for a fuel sheet, it is required."

It only took about five minutes to get the fuel and fuel sheet. When we were ready for pushback from the gate, another young male, who was a ground crewman, said he did not understand the pushback procedure. In a few decibels higher than normal, I asked him to get someone on the headset who understood. The reason I was adamant about correct procedures during a pushback was improper practices could cause bodily injury or aircraft damage. We departed 15 minutes late and flew to Denver with no problems. The next day of my four-day trip, I received a call from my flight manager questioning why I had taken a delay on my flight. Now, this was the first time I had ever been questioned about any of my procedures or decisions. No doubt existed in my mind that, as captain of the aircraft with responsibility for the safety of the aircraft and its passengers, I had conducted the flight according to FAA regulations and was correct in my actions.

The remainder of the trip gave me time to think about the situation and my flight manager's call. I was extremely upset when I arrived at O'Hare and immediately paid my flight manager a visit. We had a heated exchange, and the crux of the conversation was "making a big deal" over 15 gallons or 100 pounds of fuel was unnecessary and the company would "take care of me" if a problem existed by violating fuel requirements. I let my flight manager know I was fully aware of the small amount of fuel I requested, but I also knew Oklahoma City was a "home" of the FAA, and a flight examiner could board a plane at any time for an unannounced check ride. I was not willing to jeopardize my career on a promise.

I explained to my flight manager that I prefer to do things right the first time and not have to worry about the company taking care of me. I suggested that, instead of "ragging" me, he should make sure the 20-year-old, with only one airplane to service, put the correct amount of fuel on the aircraft. I further stated that, when I go back to Oklahoma City, if I am not 100 pounds short, but 10 pounds short at engine start, they will unload all the fuel and put on the quantity that I specified. If he wanted to accept anything less, he could fly the trip himself. I was definitely upset about this situation, and it was the only confrontation I ever had with a flight manager. When I left his office, I slammed the door, went in the outer office, and had a pleasant conversation with the receptionist and other support staff.

A Splurge to London on the Concorde

Pilots have a reputation for being cheap. Sometimes we live up to this reputation, or down to it. I would like to think of myself as frugal. Every now and then, I try to splurge a little to let Molly know I do not fit entirely into the mold of being cheap. On one trip to London, I decided to splurge and live it up.

In September 1994, I surprised Molly by asking if she would like to go on a trip. Of course, she said yes. In fact, when I ask Molly if she would like to go on a trip, she only wants to know if she needs to pack warm or cold weather clothing. She does not care where she's going—just as long as she is going. Next, I asked if she would like to go to London. Although she had been to London about eight times, she jumped with joy. Then, I asked if she would like to fly there and back from Washington Dulles Airport on the Concorde. Airline employees were offered a reduced-fare Concorde flight, and I thought this would be a once-in-a-lifetime opportunity. Molly was ecstatic and started planning and packing immediately.

The day finally arrived when it was time to leave for Dulles and our flight on the Concorde. We left O'Hare the night before our scheduled departure as we wanted to take no chances on missing this flight. We had confirmed seats—no standby for this flight. We arrived early and checked into the British Airways Concorde lounge. The lounge was exquisite with delicious appetizers and drinks served by waiters dressed in tuxedos. Our coats were collected and the next time we saw them was when we arrived in London. The airplane was small and narrow with 100 seats—all first class. We taxied out and took off for our 3-hour, 20-minute flight. In the continental U.S.A., aircraft are restricted to an airspeed of 250 knots below 10,000 feet. Once we reached 10,000 feet, the aircraft accelerated to 390 knots. When we climbed to 39,000 feet the captain said, in his British dialect, we are going into "reheat," which we Americans call afterburner, and the aircraft began to accelerate through Mach 1.** We climbed above 50,000 feet, and the aircraft accelerated to Mach 2, 1,400 mph. The highest altitude on this flight was 53,500 feet. We were above the clouds, the flight was quite smooth, and after an outstanding meal, we arrived in London in three hours and fifteen minutes.

**"Mach number: The ratio of the speed of an object to the speed of sound in the surrounding medium. For example, an aircraft moving twice as fast as the speed of sound is said to be traveling at Mach 2. The Mach number of an aircraft traveling at a given velocity depends on the altitude of the aircraft and other atmospheric conditions that affect the speed of sound near the aircraft." *The American Heritage Dictionary*

We had a wonderful, four-day stay in London, saw a couple of plays, and visited the normal tourist sights. We were not ready to leave London but were excited to get back on the Concorde. The lounge at London Heathrow had the same amenities as Dulles. When we took off and started over the English Channel, the aircraft could accelerate to the climb speed immediately since England does not have the speed and sound restraints that the U.S. does. On the flight back, the aircraft climbed to an altitude of 58,500 ft. At this height, the sky became very dark, and one could see the curvature of the earth. There is no door on the Concorde between the cockpit and the passenger cabin, only a thick curtain that passengers could not see through. The purser controlled access to the cockpit, and, during the flight, any passenger could go to the cockpit. I went to the cockpit and talked with the crew about the Concorde and mentioned that I flew the DC-10 for United Airlines. Although I knew the answer, I asked the captain if I flew the Concorde again, whom should I ask if I wanted to be in the cockpit for takeoff or landing. The captain turned around and said, "Me, of course." On European airlines the captain is the absolute authority for the aircraft. I went back to my seat and told Molly about my visit. Approximately 35 minutes before our arrival at Dulles, the purser came back and said, "Captain Norwood, Captain Smith requests your presence on the flight deck." Now, I was very cool and strolled to the cockpit. Molly has a different description about my movement and said I looked and acted VERY excited. I was in the cockpit for the final 30 minutes of the descent, arrival, landing, and taxi. With the time zones across the world, we arrived at Dulles at a time earlier than when we left London. This was truly one of the highlights of our travels around the globe.

Bill on one of his first flights as a pilot with United Airlines.

A proud Captain Norwood.

PART FIVE

Time to Land and Move On

"For once you have tasted flight you will walk the earth with your eyes turned skywards, for there you have been and there you will long to return."

—Leonardo da Vinci

On May 31, 1965, when I started my career with United Airlines, I knew my retirement date was February 14, 1996, the day of my 60th birthday. At that time, the mandatory retirement age for flying captain or first officer with the airlines was 60. That has now been extended to age 65. Through the years, and especially the last 10, I tried to psychologically and financially prepare for this date. However, as I grew older, time did seem to fly faster, and retirement was at hand.

Becoming Part of a Museum

I did not realize my retirement would be a "big deal" to anyone but me. A couple of weeks before I retired, I was asked to do print, radio, and television interviews. This was shocking and surprising to me. However, one week before retirement, I received a most memorable honor from United Airlines. My name was painted on a retired B-727 displayed at the Museum of Science and Industry in Chicago. Over 400 attended an event for the unveiling of my name. Those present included the President of the Museum of Science and Industry, United officials, family, friends, and a special group of 250 students from Chicago Public Schools. This was a tearful occasion as I spoke to the students about my "impossible dream." A plaque inside the plane has my picture and a statement stating the honor was given in recognition of my work with young people around the country.

This Boeing 727 in the museum had an interesting journey. It was flown into Meigs Airport, put on a barge on Lake Michigan, and taken into Gary Harbor. Then, it was taken to the edge of Lake Shore Drive, which had to be shut down in order for the airplane to transit from the lake to the property of the museum. Once at the museum, the plane was disassembled—the wings were taken off, the tail was taken off, and the seats were removed. One column of the museum building was removed to allow the plane to be pulled into the building. Once inside the building, the plane was reassembled, painted, and refurbished to get ready for display. I had actually flown this airplane about four times. When I go back to the museum and visit the plane, I am always humbled by this prestigious honor.

My Last Flight: a Special Day

Thirty-one years ago, when I began my airline career, I never imagined the day of retirement would come so soon. A year before that date, I came face-to-face with retirement reality when a flight attendant asked if she could work my last flight. During the last month prior to my final flight, other pilots and flight attendants began to make the same request, and it dawned on me this would be a special date and event.

My last trip was a four-day trip with the final segments being O'Hare to Cleveland and back to O'Hare. This, too, was symbolic, since my first flight in 1965 was O'Hare to Cleveland. First Officer Tony Marshall was my co-pilot for the first three days, and Captain Jim Edwards for the final two flights. My last day started with a congratulatory call from the FAA Administrator. Before we departed O'Hare, Captain Verne Jobst, with whom I had often flown as a first officer, drove an hour to the airport on his day off, came onto the plane and told the passengers they were on a historic flight. He proceeded to talk about my flying skills and the respect I had from colleagues.

On the flight, besides the regular scheduled passengers and crew, were Molly, our son George, 30 friends, 28 fellow pilots, and 13 flight attendants. Many of the pilots were from other airlines and members of the Organization of Black Airline Pilots (OBAP). Don Jiskra, United's lead photographer and videographer, was in the cockpit recording the flight, and a camera over the instrument panel recorded every facial expression. Our son, Bill Jr., was an air traffic controller at O'Hare and worked my flight from the tower.

At the terminal in Cleveland, I was greeted by family who lived in the area and several Cleveland-based employees. As I departed Cleveland, I focused all my attention on this last leg. Air traffic controllers along the way said their goodbyes and wished me a happy retirement.

When we approached O'Hare, TV stations were recording the final approach and landing and Bill Jr. was in the tower. One controller teasingly asked if I would like to make one round-trip in the holding pattern for old time sake. I laughingly declined his offer. The airspace was cleared for my 5:15 P.M. landing, and, consequently, I did not have to hold or get in line behind other airplanes. Bill Jr., cleared me to land on runway to two-seven right, the shortest runway on the airport. The wind was 320° at 8 knots, and I requested three-two left or two-seven left. He said the airport was mine and to use any runway I wished. I chose two-seven left which was longer than two-seven right. On short final, my son cleared a Continental aircraft on an intersecting runway to take off, but told him to get rolling because his dad was on his final flight, and he was not going to send him around. Then, he asked the other aircraft that were lined up for takeoff to salute the DC-10 on final approach to runway two-seven left because it was his dad on his final landing after 30 years with United. I knew most of the controllers in the tower, so I asked them if they were grading this landing. The response was that everyone had their grade sheets available. I "greased" the aircraft onto the tarmac smoothly and taxied to the gate, and the landing is all on film.

I have always been an emotional person during "sensitive" situations, and this was truly one of those times. I'm sure some even called me a "cry baby." But when I deplaned from my final flight, there was no way I could control the tears. Molly and I were both sobbing, as were many of the 400-plus people who greeted us at the gate. There were many balloons, refreshments, and a couple of brief speeches. I was interviewed by the local ABC affiliate reporter Paul Meinke, a true professional, who also interviewed Bill Jr., in the control tower. It was a great day and an outstanding way to cap my airline career.

The Party Planner Outdoes Herself

I mentioned before how Molly loves to plan parties. Well, she "outdid" herself with my retirement party. I began getting queries about when the retirement party would occur. I can't begin to say how many of my coworkers said, "Be sure to let me know when you have your retirement party." Realizing that since we had 400 attendees at my captain's party and we paid for everything, we would probably have more people attending a retirement party, and we could not pay for everything. So Molly, with the help of many, especially Ray and Patrice Washington and Beverly Jefferson West, put together an outstanding evening at the Hyatt Regency O'Hare Hotel. We wanted the party close to the airport so people who were flying in would not incur the extra expense of a rental car or a taxi ride. After selecting the menu and hiring a band, Molly decided to ask $50 per person to help cover the meal and to start a scholarship for aviation students at Southern Illinois University.

The formal invitations were mailed, and the word soon spread about the party. I had several colleagues ask if they were invited, and I would tell them to get in touch with Molly, Ray, or Patrice. One flight attendant told me she had her dress for the party but had not received an invitation. I would come home from a trip and have three or four more names to add to the list. Invitations went mainly to people who had supported me in my career. This list included not only family and friends, but the gamut of people I worked with at O'Hare and United. One interesting thing happened as we approached the date of the party. A senior captain was on the employee bus going from the airport to the employee parking lot. The captain told the bus driver he had been invited to my retirement party and since the bus driver probably would not be there, he would make sure to tell him all about the affair. The bus driver responded, "You do not have to report to me. I received my invitation three weeks ago and definitely plan to attend."

The night of the party arrived, and the attendees were dressed to the nines, with most in black tie and tux. It was a magnificent gala with 856 family, friends, colleagues, and dignitaries in attendance. The evening consisted of dinner, a short program, a professional video of my life, and dancing. The hostess of ceremonies for the program was our niece, Bonnie DeShong. She was a local radio personality and did a wonderful job. The entire evening was marvelous, but I must mention the following highlights:

- The centerpieces on each table consisted of a model DC-10 plane, spiraling through cotton clouds, and star-shaped balloons circling—no flowers.
- Molly worked with the chef, and a special mold was made for the dessert. Each guest had a white chocolate airplane filled with chocolate mousse.
- A video of my life was made by Don Jiskra, whom I mentioned previously. He interviewed family, friends, pilots, flight attendants, United officers, and even traveled to my hometown to interview my parents. The video also included segments from the event at the Museum of Science and Industry and my final flight.
- Captain Hart Langer, senior vice-president of flight operations, presented a check from United Airlines for $5,000 to begin the aviation scholarship.

- Our friend Claire Williams sang, *Wind Beneath My Wings*, and received a "tear-filled" standing ovation.
- A United States flag was presented to me. This flag had flown over the United States Capitol on February 6, 1996, the day my name was entered into the Congressional Record. This honor was made possible by the Honorable Richard J. Durbin.

To this day, we still get glowing comments about the party. I must admit it was the best I have ever attended.

Back To Our Roots

A few months before my retirement, we moved to Carbondale, Illinois. This was a bittersweet move as we had been in the Chicago area for 30 years and had developed very strong friendships. However, we were moving closer to our families. My parents, two sisters, and a brother were still in Centralia. Molly's father had passed, but her mother and one of her brothers were still in Villa Ridge. The move allowed us to spend more time with our parents as all three were over age 90. We bought a big house on 35 acres with several unique amenities, including a half-court basketball gymnasium, a regulation-size racquetball court, a Jacuzzi, an exercise room, and two family rooms. Outside we had a large, 52 feet x 22 feet swimming pool complete with a water slide and diving board. This package made our home like Disneyland Central and allowed us to entertain our family, friends, friends' children, and a multitude of others. In September 1996, Bill Jr.'s and Cindy's wedding was held in the back yard and a sit-down dinner and reception for 135 people was held in the gym. The house soon became a center for parties, reunions, and other events.

Since I was still on the SIU Board of Trustees (at that time) and we were both familiar with the area, the adjustment to our new surroundings was easy. We soon settled in, joined First United Methodist Church, and immediately got involved with community activities.

Going to Villa Ridge was always a special time for me. Since we were now only an hour away, we would go there once or twice a week. I was able to fish and hunt whenever I wished. Although Molly had never participated in these outdoor activities, she soon learned. Some of my most treasured memories in Villa Ridge were our deer hunting weekends. My brother Bobby, Bill Jr. and Cindy, other family and friends, and even Molly, often joined me for the hunts. Sometimes I would just walk through the woods and enjoy the beauty of nature, and sometimes sit on the fishing bank and enjoy the quiet peace. Villa Ridge was always a place I could feel centered and secure.

A Special Group and Another Special Flight

By the mid-70s, about 80 African Americans had been hired by different airlines. In 1976, Ben Thomas, a pilot with Eastern Airlines, met with Molly and me at our home to discuss how we could have a viable organization to benefit not only present and future African American pilots, but the aviation industry as well. (Several pilots in the New York area attempted to start such an organization in 1972, but the effort fizzled.) We put together an organizational structure with a board of directors and officers, as well as a draft of a constitution and bylaws by which the organization could operate. The main thrust of the organization would be to motivate youth, communicate with pilots among the airlines, and serve as a conduit for airline companies to hire and retain African American pilots.

Once we had completed the constitution and bylaws drafts, we notified pilots of an organizational meeting to be held at the Hilton Airport Hotel in Chicago in September 1976. Thirty-one pilots attended. It was a successful meeting; we accomplished a great deal and planned a convention for the following year.

Once the word went out about the Organization of Black Airline Pilots (OBAP), some pilots showed interest, but some were a bit "standoffish" and some airline executives were "cautious" because of the name. The organization was not excluding a pilot of any color or ethnicity who was willing to support its goals and objectives. We were not a group of radicals or a demanding group of antagonists. Led by the support of American Airlines' senior vice-president of flight, we soon eased the fear of airline executives and had the cooperation and sanction of the airlines. I served four years as Treasurer, eight years as Chairman of the Board, and six years as President. During these years, OBAP created strong and mutual relationships with the airlines.

Motivating youth was a major emphasis of OBAP. This was demonstrated through school visits, mentoring, hosting an annual youth luncheon at conventions and sponsoring summer aviation camps. OBAP also allowed me to reunite with some friends, Perry Jones and

George Nixon, who were pilots stationed with me at Travis Air Force Base but were now with the airlines.

In the spring of 1997, I had a special flight that was another "dream come true." At an OBAP Convention, a two-star general stated how proud he was of the things the organization and I had done to motivate, mentor, and assist young people into aviation. He had read about my retirement and asked if there was anything he might do for me. I expressed my desire to get a ride in an F-16, but did not hold out a remnant of hope the ride would occur.

I received a call from the Air Force asking what kind of clearance I had when I was on active duty. I provided my clearance status and Social Security number for an additional security check. About three weeks later, I received a call from the Wing Commander of the National Guard base in Springfield, Illinois. The colonel explained that he had been instructed to offer me a ride in the F-16, and asked if I were interested. I was so excited but tried to be "cool and collected" as I said yes to the ride.

I drove to Springfield and went through a brief training and medical examination. This involved a mini physical, familiarization with the cockpit, use of the ejection seat, the parachute, and other procedures involving the ride. I had about an hour before my flight so I went to the flight lounge, visited with staff, and had a light lunch including some very greasy popcorn. The colonel informed me that training had been halted for the afternoon because the wind was almost to the maximum cross wind component, but if I wanted to fly, he would take me up. I enthusiastically said I was ready to go. I was then helped into a flight suit and a g-suit**. In all of my flying experience I had never worn a g-suit.

**"A g-suit is a worn by pilots who are subject to high levels of force. It is designed to prevent a black-out and induced loss of consciousness caused by the blood pooling in the lower part of the body when under acceleration, thus depriving the brain of blood." *Wikipedia*

We proceeded to the aircraft. I was assisted in getting strapped in and identifying everything I needed to know, particularly how the ejection seat worked.

We taxied onto the runway, which was 8,500 feet long with a 1,000-foot overrun. We began takeoff, lit the afterburner, lifted off in 3,000 feet, and remained about 50 feet above the ground. When we reached the end of the overrun we were traveling 450 miles an hour. The colonel pulled the aircraft into a four and one-half G climb, my g-suit inflated around my legs, and my stomach began to feel queasy. I forgot the suit would expand with g increases. Once I realized what the sensation felt like, I began to relax. We climbed to 10,000 feet, and the pilot demonstrated the controls with a few turns, some banks, climbs, and descents. One of the most impressive things about this aircraft was that it made a 360° roll around its centerline in 1.8 seconds. He then descended to about 500 feet at 600 mph and showed me how they run attacks on ground targets. We climbed to 11,000 feet, and he asked if I would like to fly. I asked him to wait a few seconds because a couple of those horrible, greasy, popcorn kernels had come up into my throat, which I immediately had to re-swallow. I should have known better than to eat the popcorn, but the incident did take me back to my first ride in the T-Bird in hot, humid Texas.

This aircraft has a very sensitive side stick rather than a control wheel. I over controlled the craft early, but after a few maneuvers, soon settled down. Then, the colonel asked if I would like to join the "9-G" club. Of course I did. While pulling "Gs," I tightened my stomach muscles to prevent blacking out. One of the advantages of the F-16 is that the seats in the aircraft are slanted backwards, which helps blood flow. When he pulled into a steep bank, we actually pulled 9.6 "Gs." This means, at that instant, the gravitational pull was more than eight times greater than normal. I did not black out or even gray out. My vision was keen throughout this 9 "G" turn. I believe my age also gave me an advantage, since, as we get older, our blood flow slows and maintains a sufficient amount of blood and oxygen to the brain.

The colonel had a call from the base that the wind was getting stronger and we should return quickly before the crosswind limit strengthened or we would have to divert to another base. I was quietly hoping for a diversion as that would mean a second ride. However, the colonel said, "Let us return to base." He let me fly back to about 50 feet above the runway and then took control and landed. The flight was 55 minutes instead of the usual 90. He complimented me on how well I flew and said if we had been up a little longer, he would have let me land. My chest proudly expanded with this compliment. We taxied in, and I thanked the entire staff for their support and this special opportunity. Driving back to Carbondale I was reliving each minute of the flight. I had flown an airplane that I had never dreamed I would have an opportunity to fly, and this flight in the F-16 completed my flying "bucket list."

Our 40th Wedding Anniversary, Another Molly Party

All anniversaries are special, but some stand out more than others. The first anniversary is always a special time, the tenth is another milestone, and the twenty-fifth always has a warm spot in the hearts of many couples. Our fortieth wedding anniversary, on June 18, 2000, was especially important and meaningful.

When Molly first mentioned a celebration for our anniversary, my initial response was to wait until the fiftieth to celebrate. However, Molly had just finished treatments for breast cancer and wanted to have a big party. It was fortuitous and insightful to celebrate our first 40 years of marriage, because most of our family members were still able to attend. Our son, Bill Jr., was still alive, as were Molly's three brothers. So this celebration of our forty years of marriage was quite timely.

A constant in our marriage has been that that Molly loves to plan parties. When our guest list grew to over 300, we decided to rent the ballroom at City Hall for the Saturday night gala. Many of the out-of-town attendees came for the entire weekend, and Molly was excited about additional parties at our home for these guests.

The anniversary celebration was excellent. The meal was delicious, the camaraderie warm, and the evening passed swiftly. After dinner, we danced the night away with great music from a live band. Molly looked beautiful, and I was very proud to have her on my arm. The festive event and weekend were more perfect than we could have expected. Of course, as soon as the weekend was over, Molly began to plan for our fiftieth anniversary.

Bill Jr. and George

For most of our married life, Molly and I have been parents. The one thing to learn about parenting is the sooner we understand that children are individuals, the better. They are born with personalities, which can be rounded and smoothed somewhat, but not changed drastically. Bill Jr. was adventurous and liked to play on the outer edge of the circle. George was more reserved and stayed well within the rules and limits. These character traits were obvious when each of them was quite young. As a family, we spent most of our summers boating, water skiing, fishing, and traveling. Both boys were athletic, very competitive, and did well in their respective sports.

Bill Jr. (aka Roni, Ron, and Woody) always thought he could conquer any situation. Many would say he was "cocky"—he would call it confidence. He would go into any new adventure, or sport, with the ultimate belief that he would be the best. He was a good student and obeyed teachers, coaches, and his parents—most of the time. He played football, basketball, and ran track in high school. Later his passions were golf and softball. He was a very good water skier, and there is a picture of him displaying his talent on a slalom ski with one foot in the ski, the other foot holding the rope handle, and both arms stretched in the air.

During his junior and senior years of high school, he learned to fly an airplane. I had my instructor's license, and, at the time, we owned a Cessna 172, so I taught him to fly. He was a natural pilot and easy to teach. In fact, he even logged 18 minutes on a Learjet as a 17-year-old. His university career lasted a couple of semesters, and, reluctantly, he chose to go into the Army. With his background in aviation, he became an air traffic controller at Dothan Army Base in southeastern Alabama. He was an excellent controller, and during this time, the FAA was experimenting with military controllers from multi-aircraft, busy environments going straight to a local tower for on-the-job training. Bill Jr. qualified for that assignment and went directly from Dothan to the Chicago O'Hare Airport tower.

In 1996, he married Cindy Hyderall Pearce in a lovely wedding at our home in Carbondale. Molly and I became instant grandparents of Tiffany and Reed Pearce and welcomed the joy they brought, and still bring, into our lives. Bill Jr. and Cindy had two daughters, Emma and Rianna. Of course, as grandparents we have managed to spoil all four of our grandchildren.

In July, 2002, we received the shocking and devastating news—Bill Jr. was diagnosed with pancreatic cancer. As a parent, it is heartbreaking to think that your child will depart this world before you do. His courage and positive attitude were strong throughout the whole ordeal. At a family reunion in southern California in August of 2003, there was a noticeable change in his health. He, Cindy, and the girls had flown there for the reunion, and we are blessed with wonderful memories and photographs taken at Disneyland. He was brave for all of us, and the family reunion was upbeat because of him and his indomitable spirit

After two weeks in hospice, he passed on September 13, 2003. He chose to be cremated and his ashes are in the National Cemetery in Mounds City, Illinois. Unless you have walked in my shoes, it is impossible for anyone to know the pain and sorrow of the death of a child. The last thing he told Molly was, "Don't worry about me, just take care of Cindy and the girls." Every time I go to an airport, especially O'Hare, I feel his spirit and remember our times of working together.

Our daughter-in-law, Cindy, keeps us involved with our grandchildren. Molly and I realize how blessed we are to have this close relationship with Cindy. We have heard of many family circumstances where this is not the case. Tiffany, Reed, Emma, and Rianna are truly gifts from God that make my life complete.

George (aka Tony) was also athletic and excelled in academics. I am sure it was difficult at times being in his brother's shadow as I can certainly relate to that situation. In high school, George played basketball and football and participated in track and field as a high hurdler. He also played tennis and won several park district tournaments. He went to SIUC for two years, then transferred to and graduated from Roosevelt University in Chicago with a degree in business. After working a couple of years, he decided to go to Southern Illinois University's School of Law. He studied diligently and did very well there. At his law school commencement, the speaker was my longtime friend Roland Burris, who then was the Attorney General of Illinois. We both assisted in the ceremonial "hooding" of George. It was a very emotional day for me as I was so proud of how well George had performed.

After graduation, he clerked for a federal judge in South Bend, Indiana, and then worked for one of the largest law firms in Indiana for a few years. He decided to leave the firm and came back to Southern Illinois University's Law School as Director of Admissions and student advisor for one year. Then, George was appointed as an Assistant U.S. Attorney in the southern district of Illinois, where he remains to date.

George married Amy Place, the sister and daughter of friends we had known for several years. Amy is a wonderful person, and we tease her about being George's jury consultant. She attends most of his trials and is his staunchest supporter. George also co-hosts a weekly, local TV program on the PBS station on WSIU-TV. He often judges moot court procedures and serves as an adjunct professor at the SIUC law school. George now plays golf, and we have taken several golf trips together. George, like all the men in the Norwood family, is very competitive. Whether it's on the golf course or in a Wii game on television, he certainly doesn't give me any breaks for being older or his dad. What really upsets him, and is amusing for us, is when Amy wins. He definitely does not like that.

Our sons have provided treasured memories, and I am proud to be their father. I have tried to be a good and positive role model for our sons, and all young people, ever mindful of the quote by Robert

Fulghum, "Don't worry that children never listen to you; worry that they are always watching you."

Travels, Hobbies, Conquering the Canyon

The next few years, Molly and I spent much of our time visiting family in Centralia and Villa Ridge, fishing and golfing. Since we have seen most of the U.S. by air, we decided to buy a Recreational Vehicle (RV), and, during the winter, we travel to as many states as possible. We had a "fifth-wheel" that we pulled with a big truck. Molly was a trooper and soon learned to drive our "rig." Our first trip was to Florida and Georgia, and the next year we went to Texas and Arizona. We ended up buying a small "park model," basically a single-wide trailer, in Mesa, Arizona, sold our RV, and became "snowbirds." We would spend four to five months during the winter in Mesa.

I stayed current flying small airplanes. Although through the years I had owned three different planes, I did not own a plane at this time. I had several friends with planes, so I was able to fly as often as I wished. One friend in Carbondale who owned three planes approached me with the idea of having a youth aviation summer camp in Carbondale. This was something I had thought about as I had been involved in such camps through OBAP. Most of the OBAP camps were held in major cities, and I felt it would be great to bring this aviation experience to a small town and rural areas. So, with the help of many, we had a camp from 8:00 A.M. to 5:00 P.M. for five days with no charge to the students. During the week, students whose ages were in the range of 13-17 learned the history of aviation, (particularly minority and female contributions), how an airplane flies, simulator training, and flight planning. During the last two days, each student had a flight in a small aircraft and was able to handle the controls. At the end of the week, a reception was held for families and supporters to celebrate the students' accomplishments. We conducted this camp for four years and had a total of 95 students. I must comment at this point how important I believe setting high expectations are for our youth. One of my "rules" for the camp that I was adamant about was being on time. During the four years, only one student was ever late, and he was only late by two minutes.

As a follow-up to the initial camp, several students were selected to have additional instruction and soloed. From that group, one student was able to get her private pilot's license as part of the camp's goal.

Some of my friends from out of state came to Carbondale to assist with the camp; with several of them flying in their private planes. This was a gratifying time for all involved.

Another very special and memorable time was on my seventieth birthday. My friend, John Brewster, and I hiked to the bottom of the Grand Canyon, stayed overnight in the canyon and hiked back the next day. This was a wonderful experience, and words cannot begin to describe the beauty of this majestic canyon.

During the 1980s, Molly and I went on two cruises, and, while we enjoyed them immensely, we did not go on another one until 2007, when Molly's cousin, Ethel, planned a cruise through the Panama Canal in celebration of her retirement. Eight cousins joined Ethel and her husband, Dunbar, for a magnificent cruise.

Our Fiftieth: Another Cruise, Another Party

My most unforgettable cruise was to the Caribbean for our fiftieth wedding anniversary in June 2010. We decided to take our son George, his wife Amy, our daughter-in-law Cindy, and our four grandchildren on a cruise. After several friends and other family members expressed a desire to go, we extended the invitation, and the result was there were 96 people who joined us on the cruise.

The week was fantastic. Eighty-six of our guests arrived the night before, and we had a pre-cruise party at a hotel in Fort Lauderdale. The next day, chartered buses took us to the ship. All guests received bright yellow wrist bracelets to wear throughout the cruise so they could identify others within our group.

One of my favorite events of the cruise was the day we visited Dunn's River Falls in Ocho Rios, Jamaica. Our youngest granddaughter, Rianna, and I climbed to the top of the falls. I was ready to stop halfway, but she was insistent, and, of course, her wish was my command.

On the last evening of the cruise, we had a party in a reserved room. There were testimonials, laughter, tears, and dancing. To our surprise, our friend, Norma Ewing, collected $5,000 from guests for our endowment at Southern Illinois University. This was an overwhelming gift as we had specified we wanted no gifts. I cannot thank our family and friends enough for making yet another dream come true.

Since retirement, Molly and I have tried to give back to those in need of encouragement and support. With both of us having a strong commitment to education, we give scholarships annually to several institutions. We established a scholarship in Molly's parents' name for graduates at a local high school. My brother Richard, his wife Joyce, Molly, and I give an additional scholarship to students in the MedPrep program at SIUC. As I mentioned previously, when I retired, a scholarship fund was established for students in the SIUC Aviation Program from which one to three scholarships are awarded annually. We were blessed when the late U.S. Sen. Paul Simon started an endowment at the Paul Simon Public Policy Institute at SIUC in our names for the purpose of bringing speakers on race relations to the campus. I was a charter board member at the Paul Simon Public Policy Institute and continue in this capacity.

I still mentor and speak to young people whenever possible—not only about aviation but other topics as well. I heard the following saying several years ago, and it still remains on my heart.

"A hundred years from now it will not matter what my bank account was, the sort of house I lived in, or the kind of car I drove...but the world may be different because I was important in the life of a child." —Forest Witcraft

Clinton, Obama and an Honor In Lincoln's Name

During the years, I have met numerous celebrities. I would be remiss if I did not mention a few. Molly and I have had the distinct honor of meeting two sitting United States Presidents—Bill Clinton and Barack Obama. We met President Clinton in 1995 when he came to speak at SIU. We had our picture taken with him during a private reception. Needless to say, Molly capitalized on that opportunity and had Christmas cards made with her standing between President Clinton and me. The cards read, "Merry Christmas from Molly and the two Bills." We met President Obama when he was an Illinois State Senator. He was speaking in Carbondale, and I had the pleasure of playing golf with him. After golf, he came by our house, ate lunch, and gave me an autographed copy of his first book, *Dreams From My Father*. In February, 2009, Molly and I had a private meeting with President Obama when he was speaking in Mesa, AZ. I will only mention eight other individuals with whom I met and had photographs taken: The Honorable Colin Powell, Carol Channing, Coretta Scott King, Barbara Bush, Morris Dees, Martin Luther King, III, U.S. Senator Paul Simon, and

Illinois Governor Jim Edgar. I also had the honor of speaking at Senator Simon's memorial in 2003.

The highest and most distinguished honor I have received was in April, 2008, when I was inducted as a Lincoln Laureate into The Lincoln Academy of Illinois. The Academy is a not-for-profit, non-partisan organization that administers the Order of Lincoln, which is the highest honor a civilian can receive in the State of Illinois. The purpose of the Academy is:

"To honor individuals whose contributions to the betterment of humanity have been accomplished in or on behalf of the state of Illinois, or whose achievements have brought honor to the state because of the identity with it, whether by birth or residence, or by their dedication to those principles of democracy and humanity as exemplified by the great Illinoisan and whose name we bear."

I felt, and still feel, humbled to be included as a Lincoln laureate with such renowned persons as Roy Wilkins, President Ronald Reagan, Mahalia Jackson, "Studs" Terkel, Sen. Paul Simon, Gwendolyn Brooks, Mary Ann G. Morrow, and Cardinal Bernardin, to mention a few.

I believe that anyone who reads about this honor can understand how proud I was to have been a recipient of this prestigious award. I understand quite clearly that this award was a compilation of my desire, hard work, and diligence. However, I also understand that it would not have been possible without all the people who have guided, loved, mentored, and supported me and my activities through these many years. To all, I am eternally grateful.

Molly's mother had a tendency to boast about her children and their accomplishments. One time when Molly was chastising her about bragging, she replied, "It's a poor dog that won't wag his own tail." With that being said, for the sake of my grandchildren, and with Molly's insistence, I list some of the awards and recognitions I have received.

United Airlines Community Relations Award
United Flight Operations Special Achievement Award
United Airlines ORD Captain of the Year (1995)
First Edition – *Who's Who Among Black Americans*
First Edition – *Profiles in Black*
Featured in two books – *The African Americans, and African American Firsts*
Profiled in *First Edition of Chicago's Success Guide 1991*

Pictured in BLACK WINGS exhibit in the Smithsonian Institution, Washington, D.C. (This was a permanent exhibit until 2005.)
Participant in "Fifty Years of Blacks in Aviation"—Smithsonian Institute
Illinois Aviation Hall of Fame
Historical Hall of Fame and Athletic Hall of Fame—Centralia, IL
SIUC ROTC Hall of Fame
SIUC Athletic Hall of Fame
SIUC Chemistry Hall of Fame
Phi Delta Kappa Lay Leaders in Education Award
Black Affairs Council Outstanding Leadership Award (SIU)
Golden Key National Honor Society Honorary Membership
Department of Transportation Certificate of Appreciation
SIUC Distinguished Alumni Award
Service to Southern Illinois Award from Jackson County SIUC Alumni Association
SIU College of Science Alumni Achievement Award
Carbondale Lions Club David Kenney Outstanding Service to Country and Community Award
Black History Month Award (SIUC)
The Black Professional Organization, Inc. Outstanding Achievement and Leadership Award
SIU First Honorary Alumni Award (Black Aviation Association)

Life in Arizona

After much discussion and weighing the pros and cons, Molly and I decided to sell our home in Carbondale and move to Arizona. Although we had been spending the winters in Arizona since 2001, it was not an easy decision. Other than the few years in the Air Force, we had not lived out of the state of Illinois. In August 2011, we became full-time residents of Mesa, Arizona. Our home in Carbondale was replaced by a two-bedroom home in a 55-plus community. We quickly settled and found our niche in this area. I have joined the Archer-Ragsdale Arizona Chapter of the Tuskegee Airmen, Inc. It has been a joy getting involved with this historic organization and being a part of keeping their legacy and history alive. I joined two local radio control airplane clubs and stay busy flying in a different venue. We have joined the Living Water United Methodist Church and have wonderful friends in the area. Our cousins, Ethel and Dunbar Gibson, live in our community, and we spend a lot of time together. I continue to play golf, and even the hottest summer temperatures do not keep me off the course.

Not having the responsibilities of the house in Carbondale has given us the opportunity to travel more. In the past three years, we have cruised in Russia, Denmark, Sweden, Finland, Norway, Italy, Turkey, Egypt, Alaska, New Zealand, several South Pacific Islands, the Caribbean, Mexico, England, Ireland, France, and Australia. Some of our friends have labeled us "cruise junkies." This has been along with making frequent jaunts back to Illinois to visit our children, grandchildren, family, and friends.

Bill on his final flight.

Bill and his family at his retirement party—Bill Jr., Molly, Bill, and George.

Bill and family on 50th wedding anniversary cruise
George, Reed, Tiffany, Molly, Cindy, Amy, Bill, Rianna, Emma.

Molly, Bill, Emma, and Rianna.

SIU Photo

U.S. Senator Paul Simon, President Bill Clinton, Molly and Bill.

Bill, Molly and President Barack Obama.

Bill and Molly enjoying retirement in sunny Arizona.

EPILOGUE

This is my story about growing up in southern Illinois in an institutionalized, racist, and segregated society. Fortunately, my life began in a loving family with limited financial resources. My siblings and I were taught that we would have to be twice as talented, good, and prepared to be half as successful as our white counterparts. I also was encouraged to attain success by teachers, preachers, and the Centralia African American community. Encompassed in my life is a loving, protecting, and forgiving God. I had a competitive spirit, along with a determined mind and a strong belief in my talents, which aided in my challenges and quests throughout my life. I have tried to make a difference in this world by being a positive role model and helping all people. I am ever mindful of the scripture: "For everyone to whom much is given, of him shall much be required." Luke 12:48

I have been blessed beyond words—much more than I ever deserved. I am eternally grateful to all who have walked with me on my life's journey. On a recent cruise from Vancouver, British Columbia, to Sydney, Australia, I met an outstanding comedian named Frank King. Molly and I had the pleasure of visiting with Frank on several occasions, and we shared our childhood stories. When I mentioned that I was thinking about writing my autobiography, he stated, "When you were sitting on the privy, did you ever think you would ever be sitting in the captain's seat. Just think, from privy to pilot." In many ways, that sums up my life. While trying to put my life's story into print, trying to make it short and simple, I am reminded of the words of an old spiritual written by Alma Androzzo:

If I can help somebody, as I pass along,
If I can cheer somebody, with a word or song,
If I can show somebody, how they're traveling wrong,
Then my living shall not be in vain.

If I can do my duty, as a good man ought,
If I can bring back beauty, to a world up wrought,
If I can spread love's message, as the Master taught,
Then my living shall not be in vain.

WHO I AM
The Life of Captain William R. Norwood

Impossible—
dare I think or even speak
this word from beneath my breath
less I sing a song of triumph
over its defeat over its death

From the time I was a young boy
the things in life that were of true
importance to me
came with the realization
that one day, I, too, could
and would achieve —
The Impossible Dream
and to make that happen
would be no easy feat

My preparation to meet the many
challenges ahead is what propelled me
from within to do my very best
while I strove to achieve
the dreams of my quest

Through the courage
to face my ambitions and desires
I chose — to take myself higher
into another dimension of life
and explore the realities
of what seemed like an impossible life

Through the years I have been blessed
with the ability to clearly see
just what challenges lay ahead for me
and to make the right choices — in life
as I struggled and paid sacrifice

From the gridiron field of SIU
where I became a man
to the open blue sky
high up overhead
I reached — through the heavens
to touch a distant star
I thought — unreachable from afar
and embraced my destiny to become
a Pilot of the Sky

Yes, the idea to simply fly
above this beautiful earth
and freely soar
made my life all the more
exciting and challenging
as I ventured through this door

And now as I look back
I am pleased to say that much
of what I've done
would not have been possible
were it not for the strength
of my wife, family, and friends
who have stood firmly — by my side
as I've endeavored
to this end

Impossible —
No!
Nothing is Impossible

By Ronald A. Ussery

Ron is a captain with United Airlines and wrote this poem for my retirement celebration February 17, 1996.

CPSIA information can be obtained at www.ICGtesting.com
Printed in the USA
LVOW08s0844020314

375595LV00006B/8/P

9 781457 523601